U:P:D:A:T:E

Apartheid in South Africa

Third edition

David M. Smith

UNIVERSITY OF
LONDON

QUEEN MARY AND WESTFIELD COLLEGE

University of London

ii

Published by the Press Syndicate of the University of Cambridge
The Pitt Building, Trumpington Street, Cambridge CB2 1RP
40 West 20th Street, New York, NY 10011–4211, USA
10 Stamford Road, Oakleigh, Victoria 3166, Australia

First published by Queen Mary College, University of London 1983
First published by Cambridge University Press 1985
Second edition 1987
Third edition 1990
Reprinted 1993

Printed in Great Britain at the University Press, Cambridge

British Library Cataloguing in Publication Data
Smith, David M. (David Marshall), *1936-*
    Apartheid in South Africa. – 3rd ed.
    1. South Africa. Apartheid. Geographical aspects
    I. Title
    323.168

    ISBN 0-521-39720-0

Library of Congress Cataloging-in-Publication Data
Smith, David Marshall, 1936-
    Apartheid in South Africa/David M. Smith – 3rd ed, fully rev.
    Includes bibliographical references
    1. Apartheid – South Africa. 2. South Africa – Economic conditions – 1961- I. Title
    DT1757.S65 1990
    305.8'00968–dc20

Cover Illustration:
Nelson Mandela on his release from prison (International Defence and Aid Fund for Southern Africa),
segregation signs from various locations

PREFACE

The need to keep up to date with new trends and developments in geography or in aspects of geographical study is a constant problem for the teacher. This is particularly so where access to information on new techniques, ideas or sources of data is difficult and where contact with colleagues in higher education is limited. **Update** aims to confront this problem by providing brief, frequently revised booklets on topics directly linked to the 'A' level syllabus and college or university courses. The content ranges from the compilation and interpretation of up-to-date statistical information of direct use in the classroom to the discussion of recent research work which may shed new light on the received ideas of the text-book. The volumes are readable and cheap. Topics range over both physical and human geography, though coverage reflects the specialisations of the staff in the Department of Geography at Queen Mary and Westfield College, where the series is produced.

Apartheid in South Africa was first published in 1983 and revised in 1987. This third edition comprises a thorough revision, with much of the content re-ordered and re-written, as well as updated factually, to take account of the magnitude and significance of recent changes. A visit to South Africa in the summer of 1989 has enabled the author to supplement the latest statistical information and research findings with extensive field experience. Many of the maps and most of the photographs in the previous edition have been replaced by more topical illustrations. While the probability of important developments overtaking any publication on South Africa is ever present, this edition should provide up-to-date guidance for teachers, students and other readers following apartheid into the 1990s. A Postscript addresses the implications of the release of Nelson Mandela and the legalisation of the African National Congress, and points to the significance of these and related developments for the issues considered in this **Update**.

Roger Lee

Editor, **Update**

THE AUTHOR

David Smith is Professor of Geography at Queen Mary and Westfield College, University of London. He lived in South Africa for a year in 1972-73, holding lecturing appointments at the University of Natal and the University of the Witwatersrand, and spent some months at the University of Cape Town in 1979. His latest visit was in 1989, based in Durban at the University of Natal. He has also held university posts in the United States and Australia, and made a number of research visits to Eastern Europe.

Professor Smith has written or edited more than twenty books in the fields of economic and social geography. These include **Industrial Location : An Economic Geographical Analysis** (1971, Wiley, 2nd edition 1981), **Human Geography: A Welfare Approach** (1977, Arnold) and **Geography, Inequality and Society** (1988, Cambridge University Press). He is editor of **Living under Apartheid: Aspects of Urbanization and Social Change in South Africa** (1982, Allen and Unwin), and is currently preparing a new collection entitled **Urbanization in Contemporary South Africa: The Apartheid City and Beyond** for publication by Unwin Hyman. His other contribution to the **Update** series is **Urban Inequality under Socialism: Case Studies from Eastern Europe and the Soviet Union** (1989).

ACKNOWLEDGEMENTS

The author is grateful to the Hayter Fund, University of London, for a contribution towards research expenses incurred on a visit to South Africa in 1989, to the Students' Visiting Lecturers Trust Fund, University of Natal, for supporting a visit to their institution, and to the Universities of Cape Town and the Witwatersrand for various forms of assistance on shorter visits. He is particularly grateful to colleagues at these institutions, at the Universities of Durban-Westville, Fort Hare and Pretoria, and in other agencies, for the time spent with him in their offices or in the field. However, he alone is responsible for the interpretations of apartheid offered in this publication, and is aware that those with whom he worked will not necessarily share them.

CONTENTS

Preface   iii

The author   iv

Acknowledgements   iv

1. The nature of apartheid   1
    The people of South Africa
    Racial separation
    Racial inequality
    Divided government −

2. Remaking the map   14
    Population removals
    Homelands
    Group Areas
    Grey areas and open areas
    Petty apartheid

3. Explaining apartheid   30
    Separate development
  − Political domination
  − Economic exploitation
    Selective incorporation

4. Economy and labour   39
    Economic structure
    Economic geography
    Population and employment
    Labour supply
    The informal sector

5. Urban and regional development   55
    Urbanisation
    Informal settlement
    Changing urban and housing policy
    Regional development planning

6. The struggle for change   76
    Internal unrest
    External pressure
    Conclusion

Post-script   86

Bibliography and sources   88

1 THE NATURE OF APARTHEID

'The NP stands by its policy of separate residential areas, schools and institutions for different race groups.' F. W. de Klerk (as Minister of National Education, February 1986)

'The aim is a totally new and just consitutional dispensation in which every inhabitant will enjoy equal rights, treatment and opportunity in every sphere of endeavour.' F. W. de Klerk (as State President, on the opening of Parliament, February 1990)

Apartheid is dead - or so some leading Nationalist Party (NP) politicians have been asserting for more than a decade. For example, in 1984 Louis Nel, Deputy Minister of Foreign Affairs, claimed that apartheid as perceived by the outside world no longer existed in the hearts and minds of most people in South Africa, and was in this sense dead. In 1986 the then State President P. W. Botha said that South Africans had outgrown 'the outdated concept of apartheid'. Botha's successor, F. W. de Klerk, stated as early as 1978 that 'Apartheid is a word which is no longer valid and it is irresponsible to use it'. Since taking up the office of State President in 1989, de Klerk has generated a growing expectation of the creation of a new South Africa free of domination or oppression, with the release of Nelson Mandela and the legalisation of the African National Congress (ANC) heralded as major steps in this direction.

What substance is there to the claim that apartheid is being dismantled, or even that it is dead? Have major changes in the direction of racial equality really been made, with others on the way? To what extent is the government taking the lead, rather than being forced into reforms by internal dissent and external pressure? Could it be that the term apartheid is now an embarrassment, but that the state is merely seeking to restructure a system of racial domination to make it more effective or less offensive? How far is the emphasis on 'group' identity and rights, which is still evident in Nationalist Party rhetoric, simply a new code for racial privilege? Or is it really possible to conceive of a new constitution, with equal rights for all irrespective of race, arrived at by a process of negotiation? These are some of the questions raised, as South Africa enters the 1990s.

To many people the word 'apartheid' evokes racial discrimination, backed up by a repressive police state. While there is some substance to this view it is simplistic, and fails to convey the complexity of contemporary South Africa. The meaning of apartheid adopted here embraces a broad range of state policies and practices which pervade many aspects of the country's economy, society and polity. Apartheid also has a strong spatial element, appreciation of which is crucial to the comprehension of the geography of South Africa which has in important respects been recreated by government policy.

With the prospect of fundamental change in South Africa more promising than ever before, there is a temptation to look to the future rather than dwell on apartheid. However, much of the legal and institutional structure associated with apartheid still remains, along with attitudes which may be more resilient than statutes. In particular, important features of the geography created by apartheid are bound to persist in any new society, until cities and regions are reconstructed on non-racial lines. Apartheid may soon be dead, but its legacy will influence South African life for many years to come.

Rallis Preface (x)

The people of South Africa

Apartheid is a unique product of a distinctive history, which has left South Africa with a high degree of racial, ethnic and cultural diversity. White settlement began with the arrival of Jan van Riebeeck in 1652 to set up a base for the Dutch East India Company at Cape Town, but it was the British occupation of the Cape at the beginning of the nineteenth century and their immigration into what was to become Natal which really consolidated white control. While the indigenous black population of the Cape was small, much larger numbers were encountered in the interior, especially when the Great Trek took Boer descendants of the early Dutch settlers eastwards and northwards into what is now the Orange Free State, the Transvaal and northern Natal (see Figure 1.1 below for places named). A growing so-called 'coloured' population was generated by miscegenation between colonisers, the indigenous people, and Malays brought in as slaves. Further variety was introduced into the population in the latter part of the nineteenth century, with Indians imported to work the Natal sugar fields.

Shortly after the National Party assumed political power in 1948 and began the construction of apartheid, the Population Registration Act of 1950 was brought in. This required the classification of every South African according to race, the criteria being their physical appearance and 'general acceptance' or how they were regarded by others. The original Act provided for classification as 'White', 'Coloured', or 'Native' (later called 'Bantu'), but subsequent changes allowed the Indians and other smaller groups to be separated from the rest of the so-called Coloured population. Most people fall easily into one group by the official criteria, but there are marginal cases (eg people who might be considered members of other races 'passing' as White), and claims for reclassification are sometimes successful.

There are now four primary race groups recognised in South Africa. These are termed the Blacks, Whites, Coloureds and Asians. The Blacks comprise the indigenous African negro population, known officially as the Bantu until this unpopular term was abandoned in the 1970s. In liberal circles Africans is usually preferred to the official description of Blacks; the two are used synonymously here. The situation is further complicated by the fact that members of all groups considered 'non-white' (itself a pejorative expression because of its negative connotations) are increasingly referring to themselves collectively as blacks. In this publication the term Blacks with an initial capital letter is used to denote the more restricted official usage, blacks with lower-case 'b' covers all people classified as Black, Coloured or Asian. The use of capital letters for race groups, including the Whites, is to reflect the fact that these are social

constructs which owe their particular meaning to their role in South African society, rather than fixed 'natural' racial categories.

Racial nomenclature poses difficult and controversial questions in South Africa, for it can be argued that to accept the official terms is to assist in reproducing and giving legitimacy to the apartheid system. In this publication the four official terms are adopted simply because they are central to how South African society functions. Furthermore, most of the data presented come from official sources which use these race group labels. References here to parts of South Africa as 'White' denote an official connotation, without implying that such a description is either politically legitimate or accurate in a factual sense. The use of capital letters in connection with certain other terms, such as Homeland or Group Area, indicates an official designation which derives its meaning from apartheid, as will be explained in subsequent discussions.

The distribution of population by race group is shown in Table 1.1. The Blacks are in a large majority. The Whites comprise the second largest group, exceeding the Coloureds and Asians taken together by almost one million. The two sets of figures for 1988 are explained by the fact that the official definition of the Republic of South Africa (RSA) excludes Transkei, Bophuthatswana, Venda and Ciskei (the so-called 'TBVC area', after the four initials), to which the South African government has granted a form of

Table 1.1   Population by race group 1960-1988

| Race group | South Africa | | | | | | | | RSA | |
| | 1960 | | 1970 | | 1980 | | 1988 | | 1988 | |
	No 1000s	% of total	No 1000s	% of total	No 1000s	% of total	No 1000s	% of total	No 1000s	% of total
Blacks	10,928	68.3	15,340	70.4	20,886	72.5	26,974	74.9	20,613	69.6
Whites	3,080	19.3	3,773	17.3	4,528	15.6	4,949	13.8	4,949	16.7
Coloureds	1,509	9.4	2,051	9.4	2,613	9.0	3,127	8.7	3,127	10.6
Asians	477	3.0	630	2.9	821	2.9	928	2.6	928	3.1
Total	15,994	100.0	21,794	100.0	28,848	100.0	35,978	100.0	29,617	100.0

Source: **Census of Population**, 1960, 1970, 1980, and 1988 mid-year estimates. The 1980 figures for South Africa include an estimate of the population of the then 'independent republics' of Transkei, Bophuthatswana and Venda. The 1988 figures for South Africa include the 'independent' Transkei, Bophuthatswana, Venda and Ciskei (TBVC), those for the Republic of South Africa (RSA) exclude them; the small number of Whites, Coloureds and Asians living in the TBVC area are included in the Black population (SAIRR, 1989, pp. 148-9). The 1989 mid-year estimate for the total population of the RSA is 30.1 million.

independence (see next section). The result is a reduction in the Black share of the population and an increase of the share of Whites and others, when compared with the original broader definition of the national territory (referred to as 'South Africa' to distinguish it from the Republic).

Each of the four population groups identified by race is subject to internal differentiation. The Whites are made up mostly of people of British or Dutch descent; about 55 per cent are Afrikaners, by the criterion of language used at home (ie Afrikaans, a derivative of Dutch). The Coloured population is predominantly of mixed European and indigenous African ancestry, although there are also about 200,000 Malays, many of whom retain the faith of Islam. More than four-fifths of the Coloureds share with the Afrikaners their native tongue of Afrikaans. With the exception of about 11,000 Chinese, the Asians are almost all descendants of people from the Indian sub-continent, and are often referred to simply as Indians. The vast majority of Indians are English speakers; 70 per cent are Hindus and 20 per cent Muslims. The Black population is officially subdivided into ten tribes (see next section), the most numerous being the Zulu (about 6.4 million) and the Xhosa (6.2 million). Many Blacks have abandoned strong tribal identity, however, and adopted one (or both) of South Africa's official languages of Afrikaans or English.

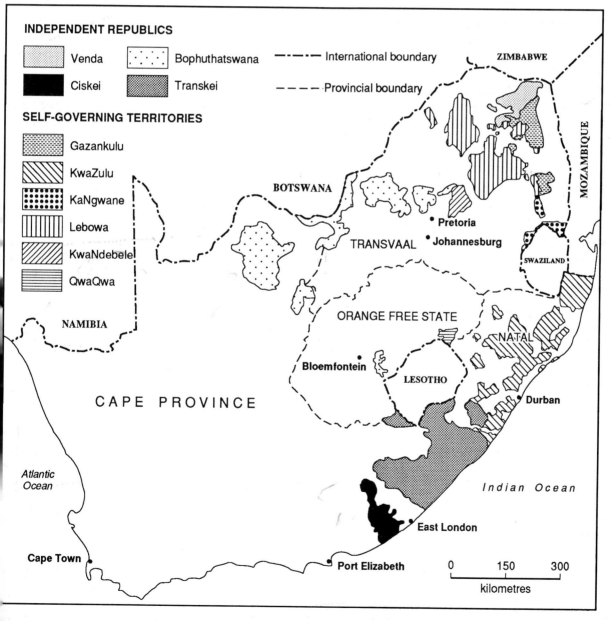

Figure 1.1   The Black or African Homelands: 'self-governing territories' and 'independent republics'
Source: RSA (1989, p. 172). Note that minor boundary changes are still taking place under the process of Homeland 'consolidation'.

Racial separation

Apartheid came about as a response to the numerical supremacy of blacks in a land controlled by Whites. The word 'apartheid' means apartness or a state of separation in Afrikaans, and the essence of the policy of apartheid is the social and spatial separation of the race groups. This operates at three geographical scales: nationally, within the towns or cities, and with respect to access to facilities. The basic principle is that race groups are assigned particular places for what is supposed to be their exclusive occupancy or use. However, the implementation of this principle differs significantly at the three different levels. What follows refers largely to former Prime Minister Dr H. F. Verwoerd's elaboration of what might be regarded as classical apartheid in the 1950s and early 1960s. Much of this remains intact today, although there have been some significant recent relaxations or reforms, as will be explained in subsequent chapters.

At the national level the territory of South Africa is divided simply between the Whites and the Blacks. The Whites have almost 87 per cent of the total surface area (for less than 14 per cent of the population) and the Blacks a little over 13 per cent (for almost 75 per cent of the population). The Black areas form a crescent around South Africa's major metropolitan region of the Witwatersrand centred on Johannesburg (Figure 1.1). When the Nationalist government introduced its policy of 'separate development' in the 1950s the areas allocated for the Blacks were called Homelands, to denote the supposed association between members of the various African tribes and their traditional areas of origin. The more derogatory term Bantustan is preferred in some quarters. The idea was that the Homelands set aside for each of the major tribal groups would eventually become independent in a formal political sense, leaving the Whites in complete control of the rest of South Africa.

The progress of this plan is indicated in Figure 1.1. A distinction is made between the four 'independent republics' as the South African government terms them, and the remaining six Black 'self-governing territories' (formerly referred to as 'national states'). Transkei was the first to be granted the status of 'sovereign independent state', in 1976, and this was followed by Bophuthatswana (1977), Venda (1979) and Ciskei (1981). However, their independence has not been recognised by the United Nations, or indeed by any country except the Republic of South Africa. The remaining six Homelands have all been granted 'full internal self-government' within the RSA, with

the objective of eventually turning them into independent republics.

There are no Homelands or specific territorial allocations for the Coloureds and Indians at the national level. They continue to reside in 'White' South Africa, ie the RSA, with the right to vote under constitutional arrangements introduced in 1984 (see next section).

The Coloureds and Indians do, however, have their allotted space within the towns and cities of South Africa, along with the Blacks and Whites. The Group Areas Act of 1950 gave legal status to residential segregation by race. This, together with the Population Registration Act, provided for the planned perpetuation and indeed strengthening of segregation in urban areas. 'Group Areas' were defined for the exclusive occupation of specific races and personal classification determined where any individual or family could legally live.

Figure 1.2 provides an example of the planned pattern of racial residential areas. Cape Town is the traditional home of a large proportion of South Africa's Coloureds (the term Cape Coloureds is still sometimes

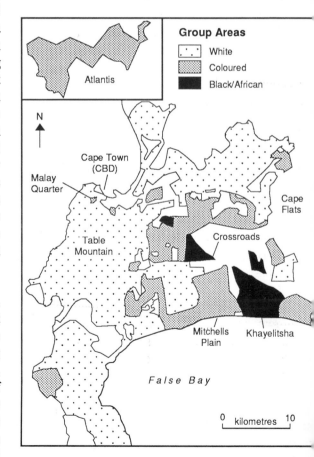

Figure 1.2   **Group Areas and Black townships in Cape Town 1985**
Source: based on A. Todes and V. Watson (in Wellings, 1986, p. 257).

Table 1.2   Population of major urban areas by race group 1985 (1000s)

Urban area	Blacks	Whites	Coloureds	Asians	Total
Cape Peninsula	282	543	1069	18	1912
Johannesburg	914	516	122	58	1610
East Rand	588	400	33	17	1038
Durban	123	308	60	491	982
Pretoria	352	432	21	18	823
Port Elizabeth	299	173	172	7	652
West Rand	387	233	19	8	647
Vanderbijlpark	352	168	15	5	540

Source: RSA (1989, p. 89). The Black population, as enumerated in the 1985 Census, is probably a substantial underestimate of the true figure, including illegal residents, in most cities.

used), and large areas are set aside for them in the Cape Flats and in the new towns of Mitchells Plain and Atlantis (40 km north of Cape Town) established in the 1970s. There is a small separate Malay Quarter near the city centre (CBD). The Group Areas for Whites include the inner parts of the city and the attractive residential districts along the flanks of Table Mountain. There are also areas for Blacks, including old-established townships and newer developments such as Khayelitsha to the east where more informal settlement is taking place (see Chapter 5). The Coloureds outnumber Whites and Blacks together in the Cape Peninsula (Table 1.2).

A second example of Group Areas is shown in Figure 1.3. Durban has the largest Indian population of all South African cities; they easily outnumber the Whites (Table 1.2). As with the Group Areas for Coloureds in Cape Town, those for Asians in Durban are peripheral, while the areas for Whites include the central part of the city and the axis through Pinetown along the main route inland. Figure 1.3 shows two different kinds of areas for Blacks: townships in the city itself as part of the province of Natal, and much larger townships of Umlazi and KwaMashu, the Homeland of KwaZulu (literally, home of the Zulu). The KwaZulu townships are effectively part of metropolitan Durban and many of their residents commute into the city daily (see Chapter 4), yet officially they belong to a separate self-governing territory which could ultimately become independent of the RSA.

The status of Blacks in South African cities requires some initial clarification at this stage. For a long time, the official position, enshrined in classical apartheid, was that the entire Black population belonged to one or other of the Homelands, in the sense that it is here that they were supposed to exercise their political rights and take their citizenship. The right to reside in an urban area was governed by Section 10 of the Natives (Urban Areas) Consolidation Act of 1945, which stated that they may claim permanent residence in an urban area only if they have lived there continuously since birth, been lawfully there continuously for 15 years, or worked there for the same employer for 10 years. This was at the heart of 'influx control', or the attempt to prevent mass movement of Blacks into the urban areas. However, the notorious Pass Laws, which required documentary evidence of 'Section 10' rights, were repealed in 1985, with the result that in some respects Black residence in the cities has become less rigidly restricted (the consequences with respect to Black settlement and housing are considered in Chapter 5).

In addition to spatial separation nationally and within the cities, the introduction of apartheid enshrined in law the traditional practice of racial segregation of certain public and private facilities. The Reservation of Separate Amenities Act of 1953 provided for the provision of public premises and vehicles for the exclusive use of persons of a particular race. Public premises include any land, enclosure, building, structure, hall, room, office or convenience to which the public has access. Land also includes the sea and seashore. Public vehicles include any train, tram, bus, vessels or aircraft used for transporting members of the public for reward. This third level of racial separation is often referred to as 'petty apartheid'.

The 1953 Act was an enabling measure, which did not itself identify facilities for the exclusive use of one race, but left this to those individuals (operating hotels, restaurants and so on) and authorities (national

6

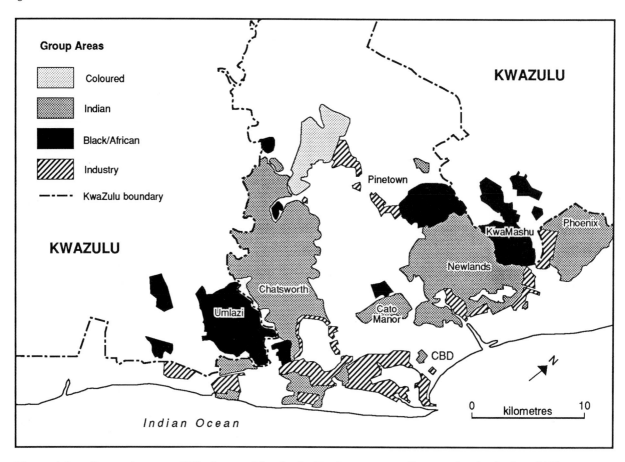

Figure 1.3   Group Areas and Black townships in the Durban metropolitan region in the late 1980s
Source: The Urban Foundation (simplified from an original map); White areas omitted.

and local government) responsible for the provision of certain facilities. Central government took the lead, with post offices, police stations and other buildings being either totally segregated or with partitions enabling blacks and Whites to be attended to separately. Civic halls, libraries, parks (and their benches), theatres, cinemas, hotels, restaurants, cafes and clubs were usually barred to blacks if in a White area. Particularly stringent controls were placed on premises selling alcoholic beverages. Sports amenities and beaches were reserved for one race group and, in some places, separate 'public' lavatories were provided for each of the four officially recognised races. Social interaction was further constrained by the Immorality Act and the Prohibition of Mixed Marriages Act, which governed sexual conduct between members of different race groups.

The implementation of petty apartheid has been considerably reduced in recent years, but still applies, in early 1990, to public schools (though not necessarily to private schools), some civic amenities such as libraries, and some bus and rail services, for example. While the last legal barriers to racially integrated sport were removed at the beginning of the 1980s, school segregation and the existence of Group Areas means that there is little inter-racial sport in practice,

and some local authorities still reserve certain facilities such as swimming pools and golf courses exclusively for Whites. Truly integrated sport requires much broader changes in South African society, and especially in the residential patterns which strongly influence where and with whom people play.

Petty apartheid has proved to be the easiest kind of racial separation to reform, although there is also some significant breakdown of residential segregation in some places. The Group Areas Act and Separate Amenities Act are both the subject of recent relaxations, further discussion of which is reserved for the next chapter.

Racial inequality

Inequality among the races is an inevitable feature of apartheid. This applies not only to the freedom to live where one chooses, to use 'public' facilities and so on, but also to a wide variety of economic and social conditions.

The most obvious manifestation of inequality is the distribution of income by race group. The top part of Table 1.3 shows that in 1987 the Whites earned 62

Table 1.3   **Distribution of income by race group 1936-1987**

Race group	1936	1960	1980	1987
Personal income (per cent)				
Africans/Blacks	18.7	19.9	24.9	27.0
Asians/Indians	1.7	2.1	3.0	3.5
Coloureds	4.2	5.6	7.2	7.5
Whites	74.9	72.5	64.9	62.0
Per capita income (Rand)				
Africans/Blacks	460	795	1,284	1,246
Asians/Indians	1,395	1,677	3,864	4,560
Coloureds	942	1,563	2,900	3,000
Whites	6,033	9,810	15,180	14,880
Ratio of per capita income				
Whites : Africans/Blacks	13.12	12.34	11.82	11.94

Source: SAIRR (1989, p. 423), after S. J. Terreblanche. The figures refer to the whole of South Africa, including the TBVC area.
1.0 Rand (R) = £0.25 approx. in early 1990.

per cent of South Africa's income (for only 14 per cent of the population), whereas the Blacks accounted for only 27 per cent of the income (for almost 75 per cent of the population). There has been an improvement over the years in the share of income going to Blacks, and also to the Coloureds and Asians, but this has been partially offset by the more rapid population growth of these groups when compared with the Whites. A measure of degree of inequality which compares the percentage distribution of income with population among the four groups, on a scale of 0 to 100 (where 0 indicates exact correspondence or perfect equality and 100 the extreme of inequality), gives the following results: 52.7 for 1960, 49.4 for 1980 and 47.4 for 1987. The bottom part of Table 1.3 shows how per capita income has changed over the same period: the ratio of White to Black income indicates a narrowing of the gap from 1936 to 1980, but there is a slight reversal in the 1987 figure. Professor S. J. Terreblanche, who was responsible for the derivation of these data, concludes that 'the relative position of the four statutory groups has changed very little' (SAIRR, 1989, p. 423).

Table 1.4 lists figures for the four race groups on a range of economic and social indicators, along with ratios of Blacks to Whites (B:W). The advantage of the Whites varies from 1.2:1 for life expectation and just over 2:1 for pupils per teacher to over 10:1 for the tuberculosis rate and almost 87:1 for manufacturing employees in professional and managerial occupations. A ratio of between 4:1 and 5:1 for earnings is confirmed by figures for individual occupational groups. The infant mortality rate among Blacks outside the RSA is unknown as many births and deaths are not registered, but a figure well in excess of 100 per 1000 live births is likely. In general, the Coloureds and Asians occupy positions between the Whites and Blacks, with Asians generally having a marked advantage. The most startling anomaly is the very high tuberculosis rate among the Coloured population, for which the Department of National Health has no explanation other than that TB is higher among all races in the western Cape where the Coloureds are concentrated.

As racial discrimination in sport attracts so much attention, it is worth noting that state spending on sport for Africans in 1988-89 came to R7.95 million compared to R8.13 million for Whites (**Financial Times**, 18 Jan. 1990, citing SAIRR data). When related to population, these figures indicate a 4:1 advantage for the Whites. It is also estimated that 90 per cent of sport sponsorship money goes to Whites. Despite some highly publicised programmes in the townships, facilities for blacks are generally very much inferior to those available to Whites.

Table 1.4   **Selected economic and social indicators by race group**

Indicator	Blacks	Whites	Coloureds	Asians	B : W
Average monthly household income (Rand) 1985	352	1958	680	1109	5.59
Average monthly earnings in non-primary sectors (Rand) 1987	593	1956	738	1061	3.30
Manufacturing employees professional or managerial (per cent)*	0.31	26.56	1.17	3.45	86.68
Maximum monthly social pensions (Rand) 1989	149.70	250.70	199.70	199.70	1.67
Infant deaths per 1000 live births 1988	62	9	41	14	6.89
Life expectation at birth (years) 1988	60	72	62	67	1.20
Incidence of tuberculosis per 100,000 population 1987	164	16	532	53	10.25
Expenditure on school pupils per capita (Rand) 1987-88	595	2722	1508	2015	4.57
Pupils per teacher 1988	41	16	25	20	2.56

Sources: South African Institute of Race Relations, various publications, from original official sources, except * from RSA (1989, p. 422). The figures refer to the RSA, ie excluding the TBVC area.

Some indication of reductions in the relative advantage of the White population in recent years is provided by comparing the ratios in Table 1.4 to those in the first edition of this publication. Monthly pensions in 1982 were 2.82:1, tuberculosis cases 1979 were 57.77:1, school expenditure 1980-81 was 6.52:1, and pupils per teacher 1982 were 2.15:1. Progress is evident, but variable. Looking further back, and comparing Whites with Coloureds, life expectation for males born in 1933-35 was 59 for Whites and 40 for Coloureds (a ratio of 1.48:1) and for females 63 and 41 (1.54:1), whereas for those born in 1984-86 the male figures were Whites 68 and Coloureds 58 (1.17:1) and the female figures were Whites 76 and Coloureds 66 (1.15:1). But there are some contrary indications: for example in 1940 the Coloured infant mortality rate, at 157 per 1000 live births, was 3.13 times the figure of 50 for Whites, whereas the ratio for 1988 (from Table 1.4) is 4.57:1.

Income and other conditions of course vary within the race groups as well as between them. The Asians and (to a lesser extent) Coloureds have emerging middle classes supplementing the small business class which has always existed in the Indian community, and their level of living is sharply differentiated from that of the rest of their race group. Even among the Blacks there is a small but growing business and professional elite. There are some poor Whites, though protected employment (eg in public utilities) and 'job reservation' (which until recently preserved certain occupations for Whites) have ensured most of them a living standard superior to that of most people in the other race groups.

A revealing commentary on economic and social conditions among South Africa's black population is provided by Eberstadt (1988), making comparisons with other countries. The 1985 infant mortality rate for the Whites was similar to those in the USA and Belgium, for Asians it was similar to those in Barbados and Puerto Rico, while for the Coloureds it was roughly the same as in Mexico and the West Bank in Israel. While the official infant mortality rate in the Black township of Soweto (28 per 1000 in 1980), if accurate, was probably lower than in the USSR, in Ciskei it has been put at about 130 - not readily distinguishable from sub-Saharan countries - and life expectation justifies a similar comparison. White adult literacy rates are comparable with those in western Europe, Japan and Australia, for Asians they are about the same as in Korea and Taiwan, while for the Coloureds the figure is, again, similar to Mexico. The overall literacy rate for Blacks, as reported in the 1980 Census (34 per cent) was lower than for any black African state and roughly equal to those in Bolivia and Turkey; the fact that it was higher (21 per cent) in the urban areas underlines the very low level of education of South Africa's rural Blacks.

Eberstadt (1988, p. 32) concludes: 'By many measures, material conditions for two-fifths of the population (homeland blacks) would seem to be scarcely better than those in a number of sub-Saharan countries commonly said to be impoverished and poorly governed'. Contrasting this with the west European standards of living of most of the Whites, and the high levels of affluence of a significant minority, effectively summarises the inequalities of apartheid.

Finally, how do people feel about their lives in South Africa? The results of surveys conducted in 1983 and 1988 (Table 1.5) show little difference in reported levels of satisfaction between Whites, Indians and Coloureds on most criteria, voting rights and job opportunities being the main exceptions. Satisfaction among Africans tends to be lower, however. Changes over the five years between the surveys suggest that perceived quality of life has decreased for all South Africans; differences between the Whites, Indians

and Coloureds appear to have been reduced, but the cleavage between these groups and the Africans has increased. The 1980s were a troubling decade for South Africans, the more so for those classified as Black.

Divided government

Government and politics in South Africa reflect the racially divided society. Although informal and to some extent formal segregation has a long tradition in South Africa, it was one political party - the Nationalists - who were responsible for the legal structure of racial separation underpinning apartheid. The Nationalists were traditionally the party of the Afrikaners, and apartheid was very much their grand design for survival as a minority population cut off from their roots in Europe. A central element in the strategy was to monopolise political institutions. From the elimination of the Coloured franchise in 1956 to the constitutional change in 1984 (see below), national politics was the exclusive preserve of people classified as White, and power increasingly the prerogative of those whose first language was Afrikaans.

From the assumption of power in 1948, the National Party (NP) steadily increased its share of seats in parliament, from 70 out of 150 to 131 out of 165 in 1981. Support for the main opposition, the United Party (UP), fell over the years, and in 1977 it was dissolved and replaced by the Progressive Federal

Table 1.5   Perceived quality of life by race group 1983-1988

| Aspect of life | People 'satisfied' or 'very satisfied' (per cent) | | | | | | | |
| | Whites | | Indians | | Coloureds | | Africans | |
	1983	1988	1983	1988	1983	1988	1983	1988
Own health	91	88	90	82	92	83	67	51
Dwelling	93	92	82	71	73	68	60	45
Public services	80	73	68	54	55	51	39	33
Family happiness	93	91	94	98	92	84	83	76
Own education	71	74	65	60	52	64	39	26
Job opportunities	66	73	37	35	47	46	19	17
Own wages/salary	70	59	55	44	57	47	26	15
Food	94	95	96	89	94	89	67	59
Voting rights	90	93	31	48	20	44	27	19
Life overall	89	82	89	77	81	77	48	32

Source: Moller (1989, p. 44), based on surveys of over 4000 people.

Table 1.6　　　　**White general election results in the 1980s**

Party	Votes			Seats		
	1981	*1987*	*1989*	*1981*	*1987*	*1989*
National	778,371	1,075,505	1,039,998	131	123	93
Progressive Federal	265,297	288,574	-	26	19	-
Democratic	-	-	430,985	-	-	33
Herstigte Nationale	191,249	61,456	5,320	0	0	0
New Republic	93,603	40,494	-	8	1	-
Conservative	-	547,559	670,723	-	22	39
Others	21,413	27,149	898	0	1	0

Sources: RSA (1989, pp. 158, 161); R.S.A. **Update**, Sept. 1989. Note that the 1989 voting figures are provisional and that the seats exclude one with a tied result, to be resolved in a new election; - indicates that the party did not contest the election in question.

Party (PFP) which was similar in its 'verligte' (ie relatively enlightened) orientation. The number of votes cast and seats won in the 1981 election are shown in Table 1.6. The voting strength of the Herstigte Nationale posed a challenge to the Nationalists from the right, ie the 'verkrampte' or hard-line racist end of the political spectrum. However, the only party other than the NP and PFP to hold seats was the New Republic, support for which was concentrated in parts of Natal.

Since 1981 there have been some significant changes in White politics. In 1982 a group of verkrampte MPs, concerned about the reforming tendency of the then Prime Minister P. W. Botha, left the Nationalists to form a new Conservative Party (CP). Some by-election successes helped to build up their strength, and in the general election of 1987 the CP polled half as many votes as the NP (Table 1.6). The fact that the Conservatives had so few seats when compared to the Nationalists is explained by the fact that traditionally much of the NP support is in the 'platteland' (countryside or rural areas) where constituency populations are relatively small and it takes fewer votes to win a seat. The decline in support for the Herstigte Nationale and New Republic parties indicated that the CP had become the natural home for most of those with anti-reformist sentiments. Superiority over the PFP in number of seats meant that the Conservatives became the official opposition.

The 1987 election marked the beginning of the end for the PFP, which had lost seats. Other groupings were forming to the left of the Nationalists, including a much publicised Independent Party led by prominent liberal defectors from the NP. In April 1989 these merged with the PFP to form a new Democratic Party

(DP), with 20 seats (ie the 19 PFP and one Independent). The DP went into the general election called for September 1989 on a platform advocating a common voters' role for all South Africans irrespective of race. The Nationalists promised 'a new South Africa', but retained their emphasis on group identity and left the political role of the Blacks for future negotiation. The Conservatives stood by traditional apartheid; they would ensure that the 'exclusive and separate community life' of the Whites would not be threatened, and refused to share power with Blacks.

The results of the 1989 election were greeted by such newspaper headlines as 'Nats hammered' (**The Argus**, 7 Sept. 1989). The Nationalists lost 30 seats. While the Conservatives gained rather more seats than the Democrats, the latter enjoyed a greater relative increase in votes when compared with the PFP and 'others' (Independents) in 1987 (Table 1.6). With 48 per cent of the total vote, compared with 31 to the CP and 21 to the DP, the NP had suffered a significant loss of confidence among White voters. But there was no clear indication of a preference for more or less reform than the government appeared to be promising.

Political party affiliation among the Whites reveals a distinct geographical pattern (Figure 1.4). Conservative support, confined to the Transvaal in 1987, is still predominantly northern and rural, with a strong challenge to the Nationalists among the traditionally conservative urban Afrikaners of relatively low socio-economic status. The NP retains control of most of the rest of rural South Africa, along with some urban constituencies. The Democrats are very much a party of the major cities, and within

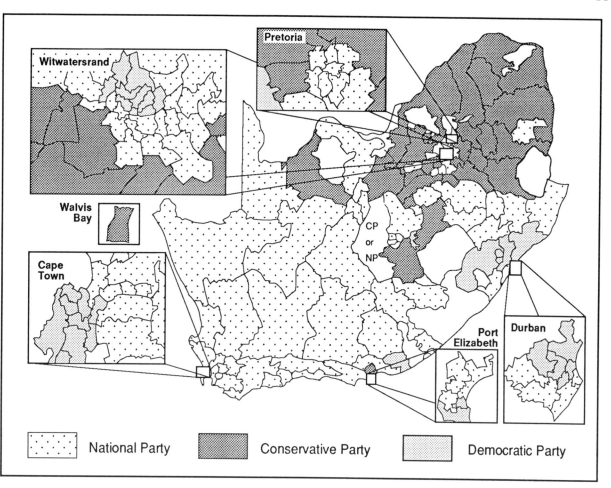

Figure 1.4   White party political affiliation in the 1989 general election
Source: South African Embassy; constituency map based on **The Argus**, 25 July 1989.

them, of the relatively well-to-do and predominantly English-speaking liberals.

The 1989 general election was the first at which people classified as Coloured and Asian were able to vote at the same time as the Whites, but on separate rolls. In 1983 Prime Minister P.W. Botha had unveiled constitutional 'reforms' which provided for a new parliament with three houses, one each for the Coloureds (House of Representatives) and Asians/ Indians (House of Delegates) as well as the House of Assembly for the Whites (Figure 1.5). There was no representation for Blacks, and power remained firmly in White hands - as indicated by their majority in the three Houses together. The new constitution was approved by 66 per cent of Whites voting in a referendum, and in 1984 the first elections to the Coloured and Indian houses were held. However, only 31 per cent of the Coloureds and 20 per cent of the Indians cast their votes.

The 1989 elections for the Houses of Representatives and Delegates revealed even lower support; only 17.6 per cent of the Coloured electorate voted and

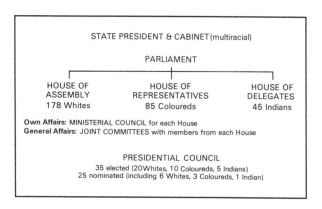

Figure 1.5   Basic elements of the constitution introduced in 1984

only 23.2 per cent of the Indians. There had been a strong campaign to boycott the election, by various organisations including the Mass Democratic Movement (MDM) which rapidly caught the popular imagination in the weeks before the election. Rather like the then 'banned' (ie illegal) United Democratic Front (UDF), the MDM stood for the transfer of power to the mass of the people so as to create a non-racial, democratic and united South Africa free from oppression and exploitation. It thus shares some of

12

the basic aims of the African National Congress (ANC).

Established in 1912, the ANC emerged in the 1950s as a mass movement advocating one-person-one-vote. It was banned in 1960 following major disturbances at the time of the Sharpeville massacre. In 1961 Nelson Mandela became leader of Umkhonto we Siswe ('Spear of the Nation'), the newly formed military wing of the ANC; he and some of his associates were subsequently put on trial and sentenced to life imprisonment in 1964. The ANC has greatly increased its influence in recent years, as a rallying force for opposition to continued White rule, and its legalisation along with the release of Nelson Mandela in February 1990 ensures the organisation a prominent role in negotiations towards a new constitution.

To opponents of apartheid, the 1984 constitution is unacceptable, because it continues to enshrine racial separation and differentiation. A crucial distinction is made between 'general affairs' affecting all race groups, which are considered in all three houses, and 'own affairs' which are deemed to concern a specific race and are therefore the subject of debate only in the house of the group in question. Affairs regarded as general are supposed to be resolved by consensus, making use of joint committees comprising members of each house. If no consensus can be reached the final decision is made by the President's Council, on which a White majority is guaranteed by its representation and by the President's power of nomination. The major innovation of the new constitution, apart from the incorporation of Coloureds and Indians, was their representation in both Cabinet and Presidential Council. However, racial identity is a central feature of the entire structure, reinforced by the concept of 'own affairs' which are taken to include a wide range of matters relating to social services, recreational and cultural facilities, housing, community development and local government.

Some consideration was subsequently given to ways of incorporating Blacks/Africans, and to the reform of other levels of government and administration. For example, a National Council was proposed as a means of involving Blacks nationally, via representatives of the Homelands, and possibly of

*Opposition to the 1989 general election to the three racially separate houses of parliament: **Plate 1** (left) call from the Natal Indian Congress not to vote, with posters for candidates in the Clairwood district of Durban; **Plate 2** (right) shop in Mitchells Plain, the large town built for Coloured people in the western Cape, observing closure organised by the Mass Democratic Movement (MDM) on election day.*

townships in 'White' South Africa, although this was not followed through. New councils were established at the provincial level, however, for the Cape, Natal, Orange Free State and Transvaal, including nominated representatives of 'non-white' groups. Regional Service Councils are bringing together representatives of racially separate local authorities on multi-racial bodies concerned with the provision of certain services and aspects of development planning (their significance is considered further in Chapter 5). Within the cities, Black Local Authorities provide a degree of control over Black 'own affairs', though elections are very poorly supported.

While these developments represent some relaxation of White monopoly over government at all levels, they retain the basic geo-political structure of 'White' South Africa, Black Homelands and racially homogeneous local communities. A more radical alternative emerged in 1986 from the so-called KwaZulu-Natal 'Indaba' (conference), involving discussions between Whites, Indians and Blacks, which proposed what was, in effect, a merger of 'White' Natal and the KwaZulu Homeland under a constitution which could bring Black majority rule.

Government opposition to something so clearly inconsistent with their own limited conception of power-sharing was made clear, although the geographical logic of a KwaZulu-Natal makes it a continuing source of debate, in its own right and as a possible model for geo-political reorganisation elsewhere in South Africa.

The fundamental question of Black involvement in national politics is still unresolved, however. The Nationalists went into the 1989 election committed to finding a new constitutional system in which all races would participate and no group would dominate the others. Having been the dominating group, the Whites must not in future be among the dominated, according to this Nationalist vision. At the time of writing, the new session of parliament has opened with the government attempting to set up a process of negotiation with the ANC and other representatives of the Black population. The release from prison of Nelson Mandela, personification of the Black liberation struggle for the past quarter of a century, was a crucial if preliminary step in this process, the latest implications of which are outlined in the Post-script to this volume.

2 REMAKING THE MAP

P 29 of this Book

'If I were to wake up one morning and find myself a Black man, the only major difference would be geographical.' (B. J. Vorster, as Prime Minister, April 1972)

The creation of apartheid has been described as an ambitious exercise in applied geography. The map of South Africa has been redrawn in significant respects, to give substance to a racial application of the old adage of 'a place for everyone, and everyone in their place'. Indeed, geographical position is the only thing that is supposed to make a difference between people defined by race group, according to traditional apartheid ideology. Blacks and Whites are supposed to have the same rights and responsibilities, but in different places.

This chapter considers the implementation of the policy of racial separation at different spatial scales, how far it has proceeded, and 'succeeded' in its own terms, along with some recent reactions and reversals. As well as the broad facts, case studies have been selected to reveal some of the local impact in more detail.

Population removals

The creation of racial separation at the national and city scales has required the relocation of large numbers of people. Accurate figures are difficult to obtain, but an estimate cited by the Black Sash Organisation puts it at approximately 3 million people from 1960 to 1980, while a study by the Surplus People Project (Platzky and Walker, 1985) arrived at 3.5 million for these two decades. Some other estimates put the figure higher, for example a minimum of 4 million if unrecorded involuntary moves are included (see Unterhalter, 1987, for details).

Table 2.1 shows the number of people (mostly Blacks/Africans) involved in various types of removals or relocations according to the Surplus People Project - the most comprehensive study yet undertaken. The first category refers to changes in the way in which Africans could work on the land in 'White' South Africa. Under the Natives' Land Act of 1913, Africans hiring, leasing or owning land outside their scheduled 'reserves' (which later became the Homelands) were said to be squatting illegally in 'White' areas. Subsequently large numbers of squatters and labour tenants (working part of the year

for white farmers in return for land and grazing rights) have been resettled in the reserves or Homelands, a process accelerated by agricultural mechanisation in the 1950s and 1960s.

The term 'Black spots' describes parcels of land bought freehold by Africans before the 1913 Act. The elimination of 'Black spots' is an important feature of the consolidation of the Homelands. As the land involved has often been owned and farmed by the same Black families for generations, forced resettlement in what can be a far distant Homeland is a source of great hardship. The number affected approaches 0.7 million. Almost 1 million more Africans were subject to removal from the remaining 'Black spots' and other areas, under the 1975 proposals to reduce the number of separate Homeland territorial units from over 100 to less than 30.

In the urban areas the demolition of old so-called locations or townships, 'shanty towns' and other 'unauthorised' settlements, along with the creation of Group Areas, has resulted in the movement of large numbers of people (Table 2.1). Some have been rehoused in new townships, others relocated in the Homelands, while many have formed new spontaneous 'shack' settlements (as described in Chapter 5). Blacks have also been removed from 'White' cities if they became 'unproductive' (eg too old or ill to work) or otherwise lost their residence rights, and in cases where they were officially regarded as 'undesirable' (eg political activists).

P 62

During the early 1980s African removals continued at a level of 20-30,000 per year. In mid-1986 the government announced that it would not proceed with hundreds of thousands of outstanding removals, but resettlement continued and rose to 64,180 in 1986 and 47,617 in 1987 according to government sources. These official figures alone (likely to understate the true magnitudes) put the total African removals since the Surplus People Project (ie from 1981 to 1987) at just over 250,000. In 1988 the government announced plans to move a further 248,000 Africans in 60 communities by 1995 (SAIRR, 1989, pp. 171-3). The long history of residential insecurity for African people thus continues.

Homelands

The Homelands or Bantustans were introduced in the previous chapter, along with the distinction between

Table 2.1   Population affected by removal or relocation c. 1960-1980

Type of removal	Numbers
Eviction of Black tenants, squatters and surplus labour from 'White' farmland	1,129,000
Clearance of 'Black spots', and Homeland consolidation	647,000
Urban relocation and removal from 'White' areas to Homeland townships	670,000
Removal from unauthorised (informal or spontaneous) urban settlements	112,000
Group Areas removals arising from racial re-zoning	834,000
Relocation due to development schemes and clearing sensitive areas	23,500
Political moves such as banishment and flight from oppression	50,000
Others	30,000
Total	3,522,900

Source: The Surplus People Project, as reported in SAIRR **Race Relations News,** May/June 1983. Some of these figures may be underestimates; for example, other evidence suggests a larger number of people affected by removal from informal settlements, and a Stellenbosch University study in 1986 reported at least 4 million Blacks relocated into the Homelands between 1951 and 1980.

those considered 'independent' and those with 'self-governing' status within the RSA (see above, Figure 1.1). The territorial disaggregation of the original state of South Africa was set in motion by the Black Self-Government Act in 1958, shortly before South Africa itself left the British Commonwealth and became a republic in 1961. It was envisaged that a number of nation states based on the historic territories of the various Black tribal groups could satisfy the political aspirations of all Black people, no matter where they lived. In 1963 Transkei, the Homeland of the largest section of the Xhosa people, was granted 'full internal self-government', with a legislative assembly which could pass laws on most matters of immediate concern to the people of Transkei (eg agriculture, public services and administration). The territory was also granted some of the customary symbols of nationhood, such as its own flag and anthem, and Xhosa joined Afrikaans and English as an official language.

Subsequently, all the remaining nine Homelands were granted self-governing status (Table 2.2), a process completed with KaNgwane in 1984. In 1976 Transkei became the first to be granted what is supposed to be full independence as a sovereign state, with its own constitution determined by the people of Transkei themselves. Three others had followed by 1981, to form the so-called TBVC area or states. In a simple geographical sense, what has been achieved so far may be judged against two criteria: the territorial basis established for the Homelands, and the extent to which they have incorporated their particular tribal populations.

The broad territorial basis for the Homelands goes back to 1913, when the South African parliament scheduled about 9 million hectares of land mostly occupied by Africans as inalienably African property. Under the Native Trust and Land Act of 1936 this was increased to 15.3 million hectares, including about 5 million which would have to be purchased, mainly from White farmers, over an indefinite time period. The 1936 Act still provides the basis on which the allocation of land to self-governing and 'independent' territories is arrived at, although some additional land has subsequently been provided.

The practical problem of Homeland consolidation arose from the scattering of land occupied by Africans (not all of which was destined for incorporation) and from the position of other land to be acquired. Consolidation proposals accepted by parliament in the 1970s reduced the total number of component land units from 98 to 28. However, the process of consolidation has been slow and contentious, and the number of individual units of land is still well above what was proposed. For example, in 1988 government plans for KwaZulu, the most fragmented of the Homelands, aimed at reducing its 26 separate areas to 19 (SAIRR, 1989, p. 91). The Homelands together comprised almost 17 million hectares, or 13.8 per cent of the land of South Africa including the TBVC area (Table 2.2).

The total population of the ten Homelands is almost 14 million (Table 2.2). As this is only slightly more than half the Black population of South Africa as a whole, there is obviously a major discrepancy between

Table 2.2   The Homelands ('independent republics' and 'self-governing territories')

Name (tribe)	Date of 'self-governing' ('independent') status	Size 1987 (1000s hectares)	Popul- ation 1988 (1000s)	'Citizens' outside in RSA 1985 (1000s)
Transkei (Xhosa)	1963 (1976)	4,287	3,168	683
Bophuthatswana (Tswana)	1972 (1977)	4,187	1,870	589
Venda (Venda)	1973 (1979)	708	503	89
Ciskei (Xhosa)	1972 (1981)	794	822	331
Lebowa (North Sotho)	1972	2,213	1,991	619
Gazankulu (Shangana/Tsonga)	1973	765	539	178
QwaQwa (South Sotho)	1974	72	197	704
KwaZulu (Zulu)	1977	3,184	4,061	1,121
KwaNdebele (Ndebele)	1981	291	256	212
KaNgwane (Swazi)	1984	438	425	330
Total		16,945	13,830	4,857

Source: SAIRR (1989, pp. 51, 86, 148). Note that the figures for size are subject to continuing change with the process of consolidation. Population figures for 1988 are based on 1985 Census data and an assumed subsequent annual growth rate of 2.8 per cent, except for its own estimate in the case of Venda. The number of 'citizens' in the RSA is an estimate by the Minister of Home Affairs, and does not include all Blacks living in the RSA.

the Homeland to which people have been assigned on a tribal basis and where they actually live, despite the massive population removals reflected in Table 2.1. Census figures for 1980 showed only 48 per cent of the total Black population living in their tribal Homeland, a proportion which ranged from 63 per cent in Venda to as low as 11 per cent in the minute QwaQwa which could not physically accommodate anything approaching the complete South Sotho population of 2 million.

Since 1980 the 'independence' of the TBVC states and their consequent excision from the Republic of South Africa, procedures for recording population have changed and made calculations more difficult. However, Table 2.2 shows almost 5 million Homeland 'citizens' resident outside, in the RSA, in 1985. Figures from the 1985 Census for the tribal groups of the six Homelands still within the RSA show 67.5 per cent of Zulu living in the Republic resident in their Homeland, 65.7 per cent of North Sotho, 43.9 per cent of Tsonga, 43.4 per cent of South Ndebele, 30.7 per cent of Swazi, and a mere 8.6 per cent of the South Sotho in QwaQwa. As to the 'independent republics', South African government figures in 1987 showed almost 1.8 million TBVC 'citizens' permanently resident in the White republic, including 733,000

from Transkei, 599,000 from Bophuthatswana, 336,000 from Ciskei and 95,000 from Venda (SAIRR, 1988, p. 854), and such figures are bound to be underestimates of the actual Black population in the 'White' Republic.

The relocation of Black people to the Homelands has been at enormous cost in terms of human suffering. Both urban and rural communities have been broken up, and forcibly removed to places with which they no longer have any association. The plight of people dumped in what were often remote, inhospitable and infertile resettlement areas was first highlighted by Father Cosmas Desmond (1971); almost two decades later such places are still characterised by primitive living conditions and lack of local means of making a living.

Figure 2.1 provides one illustration of the process of Black resettlement, in connection with the consolidation of the Tswana Homeland of Bophuthatswana, now officially an 'independent republic'. Some of the distances moved are well over 100 miles. Population relocation can also involve the transfer of people living in the Homelands but of the 'wrong' tribe. Examples on the map are the removal of non-Tswanas from the section of Bophuthatswana

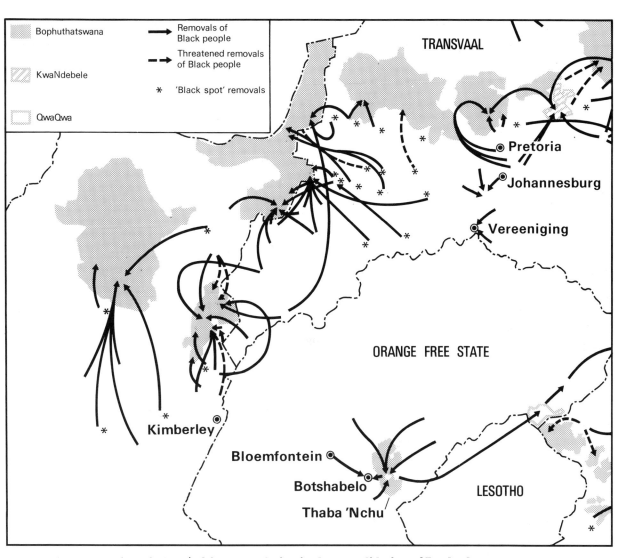

Figure 2.1   Relocation of Black/African population in the consolidation of Bophuthatswana
Source: section of map in Walt (1982).

north of Pretoria to KwaNdebele and from Thaba 'Nchu to QwaQwa. Bophuthatswana is the major exception to the general tendency for tribal homogeneity within individual Homelands; at the 1980 Census the recorded population of Bophuthatswana exceeded its Tswana population by about 400,000, and the government of this Black state has played a prominent and not always gentle part in 'encouraging' non-Tswana to leave for their own Homeland.

One recent case may be used to show the geographical absurdity of tribally homogeneous Homelands taken to the extreme. Botshabelo (formerly known as Onverwacht) is a settlement of about half a million people which has formed over the past decade, largely as a result of the displacement of Blacks from White-owned farms and deproclaimed townships in the Orange Free State. It is the largest 'relocation slum' in the country (Murray, 1988, p. 114), and second largest Black town after Soweto. Its population is

about 70 per cent South Sotho. In 1987 Botshabelo was incorporated into the South Sotho Homeland of QwaQwa, whose own population of about 200,000 comprised the other main concentration of this tribal group. QwaQwa is 330 km away, yet Botshabelo actually adjoins the detached Thaba 'Nchu area of Bophuthatswana (see Figure 2.1). The incorporation of Botshabelo into QwaQwa was strongly opposed by many of its residents, and subsequently declared invalid by the South African Supreme Court. However, the government gave notice of intent to appeal, and at the time of writing the matter is still unresolved. The main achievements of incorporation would be greatly to increase both the size of QwaQwa, prior to possible 'independence', and the proportion of South Sotho people living in their supposed Homeland no matter how strange its geographical disposition.

The so-called 'independent republics' have adopted certain of the expected institutions and symbols of

*Two sides of the 'independent' Homeland of Ciskei: **Plate 3** (l) modern shops and office complex in the capital, Bisho; **Plate 4** (r) resettlement area at Msobomvu for Africans evicted from White farms or 'Black spots' in the eastern Cape.*

conventional sovereign states. Each has its seat of government and capital city, the construction of which gives (literally) concrete expression to the way in which the states themselves and the South African government would like the rest of the world to see them. Take Ciskei, for example. Instead of transferring the (White) historic capital of the region, King William's Town, to Ciskei, the RSA built a new capital called Bisho only a few kilometres away. Three villages had to be resettled, at a cost of R6.1 million. Expenditure on construction has been vast: an estimated R59 million by the end of 1987 with a R20 million civic centre completed in 1988 (B. Streek, in Van der Kooy, 1988, p. 62). By 1989 Bisho boasted a casino and shopping centre, as well as the Ciskei House of Assembly, Presidential palace and private house, large houses for government ministers and civil servants, government departmental offices, courthouse, church and private school. There is also a R25 million 'international' airport which has not yet been used, and a Ciskei International Airways with jets which have yet to fly. Ciskei is one of the poorest regions in South Africa.

Group Areas

The creation of racially homogeneous residential areas in the cities has affected all race groups, the more so those who are not Whites. By the end of 1987, 1321 Group Areas had been proclaimed in all, 576 for the occupation of Whites, 495 for Coloureds and 250 for Indians (Black residential areas are traditionally 'townships', not Group Areas in the strict sense). The fact that Group Areas were still being created, despite growing opposition and non-compliance (see below), is shown by the fact that 19 new ones were proclaimed in 1986 and 33 in 1987.

Table 2.3 shows something of the impact of Group Areas, borne disproportionately by the Coloureds and Indians, with few Whites affected. The cost to Indian businesses moved from areas proclaimed for Whites has been severe. People affected by relocations under the Group Area Act include the equivalent of one-third of the entire Indian population and one-sixth of the Coloureds; the total exceeded 800,000 by 1980 (Table 2.1) and a figure of one million to date would not be much of an exaggeration.

The extent to which the implementation of Group Areas may have achieved racial residential segregation is suggested in Table 2.4. This includes areas set aside for Black/African residence. The vast majority of South Africa's urban population officially lived in its 'own' Group Areas in 1985; only 10 per

Table 2.3   Families and businesses affected by the Group Areas Act up to 1984

Category	Whites	Coloureds	Indians
Families moved, up to August 1984	2,418	83,691	40,067
Families remaining to be moved	258	3,790	2,366
Businesses relocated, up to 31 August 1984	54	187	2,530

Source: SAIRR (1986, pp. 348-9). In September 1984 responsibility for removals became an 'own affair' within the tri-cameral constitutional system; the administrations concerned claim that removals since then have been negligible (SAIRR, 1988, p. 502).

Table 2.4   **Urban population (1000s) by race group and Group Area of residence 1985**

Race group	Group Area of residence					Per cent in own Area
	White	Coloured	Asian	Black	Total	
White	4,078.6	6.4	2.3	4.7	4,092.1	99.7
Coloured	189.0	1,978.3	17.3	48.0	2,232.6	88.6
Asian	44.8	10.8	710.2	1.7	767.5	92.5
Black	820.2	24.1	25.6	4,027.5	4,897.4	82.2
Total	5,132.7	2,019.6	755.4	4,081.9	11,989.6	90.0

Source: Christopher (1989, pp. 264-5; figures rounded).

cent of the total were in the 'wrong' place. The greatest extent of conformity is on the part of the Whites, the least by Blacks almost one-fifth of whom live in other Group Areas. However, these are Census data, which will have failed to record many blacks living illegally in White Group Areas (see below).

Three cases, involving each of the largest cities, may be used to illustrate the impact of the creation of Group Areas. The first concerns Cape Town, where the Group Areas as proclaimed in 1985 were illustrated in Chapter 1 (Figure 1.2). Figure 2.2 shows the highly diverse ethnic residential pattern at the beginning of the apartheid era, revealing in particular the intermingling of small Coloured and Malay enclaves within the predominantly 'European' areas around the foot of Table Mountain. The Group Areas as established by 1979, for those other than Whites, show most of the old Coloured and Malay areas relocated into the Cape Flats. All that remains are the historic Malay Quarter to the south-west of the CBD and Walmer Estate on the edge of District Six.

District Six (named after the old sixth district of Cape Town) has become especially symbolic of the impact of the Group Areas Act. Closely associated with the history and culture of the Coloured people, the area developed a vibrant, cosmopolitan but impoverished community, and at one time had a population of about 60,000. In 1966 District Six was proclaimed White under the Group Areas Act, a move which was imposed by the national government in Pretoria over the objection of the City of Cape Town. Most of the area was subsequently cleared, its houses demolished and its Coloured population relocated in the Cape Flats (for details see Western, 1981; Hart, 1988). In 1979 District Six was officially renamed Zonnebloem, as if to complete the elimination of its former existence and identity. However, the expected reoccupation of District Six by Whites has been constrained by a feeling that this is tainted ground, and much of it still remains vacant today. The final irony is the

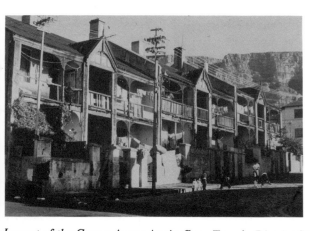 

*Impact of the Group Areas Act in Cape Town's District Six: **Plate 5** (l) old property of the type demolished when the Coloured people were moved out; **Plate 6** (r) land close to the city centre left vacant after clearance in the 1970s and still largely unoccupied today.*

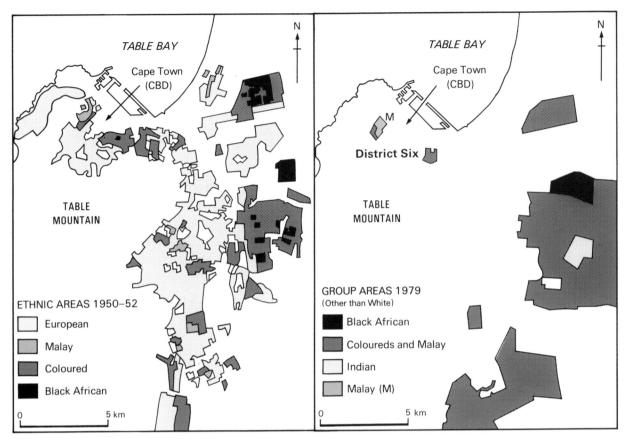

Figure 2.2   **The distribution of ethnic groups in Cape Town on the introduction of apartheid, and subsequently proclaimed Group Areas**
Source: Western (1981, pp. 51, 104).

government's designation of District Six in 1989 as one of the first 'Free Settlement Areas', open for the occupation of all race groups (see below).

The second case is from Durban, the Group Areas of which were shown in Chapter 1 (Figure 1.3). Before the era of apartheid the Whites and Indians occupied their own highly segregated residential areas, with the Whites concentrated along the Berea ridge to the west of the CBD and the Indians just beyond. Within the CBD the Indians had their own mixed residential and commercial area based on Grey Street (Figure 2.3). The designation of Group Areas for the Indians broke up their old communities and forced them into more peripheral locations, leaving the central parts of the city firmly in White control. Whereas most Indians originally had their own houses on freehold land, most now live in rented property. There has also emerged a form of socio-economic segregation which hardly existed before; now the better-off Indians have their own separate areas of fine homes in Westville, for example, distinct from those of the large majority in Chatsworth and Phoenix. The implementation of Group Areas thus accommodated and even accentuated class differentiation within the Indian community, assisting socio-economic segregation of the kind found in more 'normal' societies.

The treatment of the Grey Street business district was similar in some respects to that of Cape Town's District Six. The Whites had long been concerned about competition from Indian traders, and various formal and informal means were used to protect White businesses before the apartheid era. But Grey Street represented Indian business success in a conspicuous inner-city location. In 1973 Grey Street was proclaimed an area for Indian businesses but not for residence. The significance of the distinction was that many businesses were family-run and residential accommodation was often integral (literally, over the shop); thus the viability of Indian business was threatened indirectly. Between 1973 and 1981 the resident population of the Grey Street area dropped from 13,000 to 6,500, with implementation of the business-only proclamation, but the area has survived and continues to prosper as a distinctively Indian business district.

The third case concerns Johannesburg. Before the apartheid era there were substantial pockets of African population around the inner city, as well as Coloured and Indian communities. Figure 2.4 shows the Black townships and so-called 'slumyards' in 1930, and the subsequent process of relocation to the massive South Western Townships now known as Soweto. Alexandra, to the north of the city, is the sole survivor

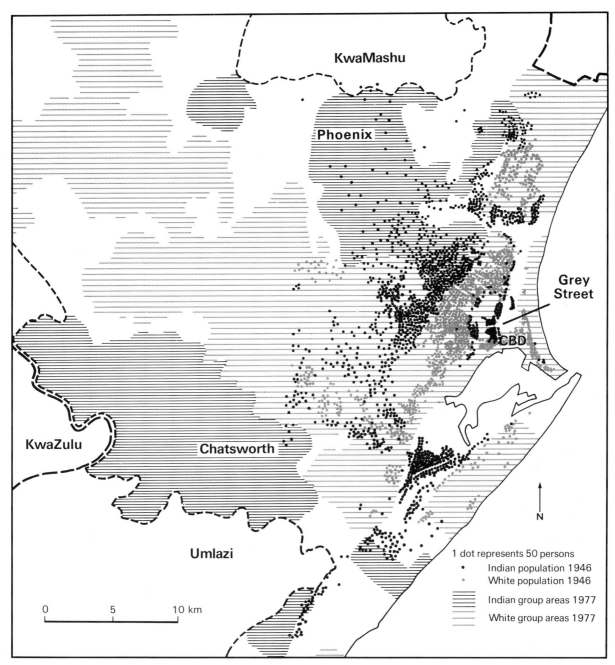

Figure 2.3 **The distribution of Indian and White population in Durban on the eve of apartheid, in relation to Group Areas**
Source: Maasdorp and Pillay (1977, p. 24).

today. The map of Group Areas shows that the major provision for the Coloured and Indian populations is in the peripheral districts of Eldorado Park and Lenesia respectively, though there are smaller areas closer in. White residential space is distinct and separate. It is also much less densely occupied: figures for 1985 show only 15 Whites per hectare of proclaimed land, compared with 29 for Asians, 50 for Coloureds and 105 for Blacks (Christopher, 1989, p. 256).

Just as the other cities have their symbolic victims of the Group Areas Act, so does Johannesburg. Sophiatown is a case in point. Established in 1905

north-west of the city centre, Sophiatown offered freehold occupancy for Blacks, and attracted a growing population as other residential opportunities became severely restricted. By the beginning of the 1950s there were over 60,000 residents, and the district had become severely congested. Sophiatown was destroyed as 'slum clearance' between 1955 and 1962, and replaced by a residential area for Whites appropriately renamed Triomf ('Triumph' in Afrikaans). What was lost in the process was not only conveniently located accommodation for Blacks, but also a distinctive local community which contrasted strongly with the newly created townships such as Soweto. As Hart and Pirie (1984, pp. 44-5)

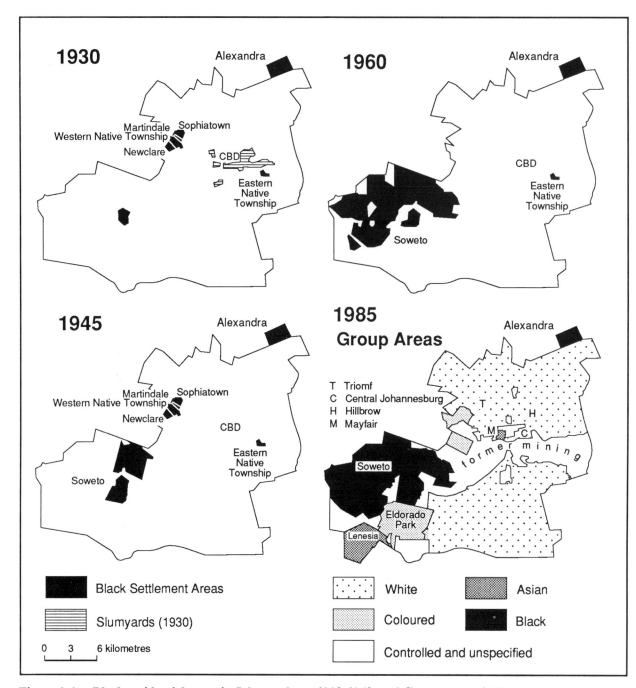

Figure 2.4   Black residential areas in Johannesburg 1930-1960, and Group Areas 1985
Sources: residential areas from C. Rogerson and D. Hart, (in Welling 1986, p. 154); Group Areas from Christopher (1989, p. 257).

describe it:

Sophiatown boasted vitality and exuberance that were not found in other South African suburbs. ... The bustle and variety of Sophiatown were instrumental in making it a lived-in place, not just a labor entrepot. ... The soul of Sophiatown was identifiable not only by its unique attributes but also in contrast to the soulless, municipally controlled, black urban 'locations', the qualities of which were intimately shaped by memories and expectations of Sophiatown.

... The regimental locations with their bland generic label conveyed a sense of placelessness and unbelonging that helped emphasize the peculiar embrace of Sophiatown.

Population removals under the Group Areas Act were often justified by the authorities as slum clearance in the interests of public health. Many of the areas concerned were overcrowded, with poor housing and insanitary conditions. The quality of accommodation into which people were moved may

Contrasting Indian areas in the Witwatersrand: **Plate 7** *(l) Dikthole, a former inner-city business district, where sewage disposal is still by truck;* **Plate 8** *(r) homes of the well-to-do in the peripheral township of Lenesia .*

have been superior to the original in some physical respects, but there was a loss of broader community and environmental quality. For example, in the Cape Flats human relationships became more impersonal, social deprivation more evident and personal safety less secure than in the traditional Coloured areas of Cape Town (Western, 1981). In some of these older areas the housing was structurally sound if superficially dilapidated, and the Group Areas Act generated benefits for some Whites as former Coloured homes were bought up cheaply and renovated to create fashionable residential areas with easy access to the city centre.

Far from creating separate but equal conditions, as envisaged by some of the early architects of apartheid, residential segregation by race has been accompanied by stark differences in the quality of housing and local services. Something of the reaction on the part of people consigned to areas other than those for Whites is indicated by the following extract from a letter written by H. Budhram, an Indian councillor, to a Durban newspaper (**Daily News**, 5 Aug. 1989):

> It is time that Durban City Council stopped evading its responsibilities towards the voiceless citizens. The deplorable state of some of the Indian coloured and black residential areas with narrow, undeveloped filthy roads, poor drainage systems, untrimmed verges, dilapidated bus shelters, lack of playlots, libraries, community centres and infrastructure for the development of vacant plots, are not only an eyesore in themselves but a painful reminder of the blatant discrimination and injustice on the part of those who are vested with authority to dictate our lives. Notwithstanding the fact that 70 per cent of the rate payers in Durban are Indians and coloureds, most of their residential areas are in an appalling condition.

The point is that the concept of Group Areas was imposed by national political institutions from which the Asian, Black and Coloured population had been excluded, and has been implemented within local government structures dominated by the Whites. It is also a reflection of racist thinking, in which some people are considered inferior to others and therefore entitled to an inferior quality of life.

Grey areas and open areas

Recent years have seen a significant breakdown of the strict racial residential segregation required by the Group Areas Act. The term 'grey areas' is applied to places designated for a particular race group under the terms of the Act, but which are nevertheless to some extent integrated. The 'greying' process usually applies to White Group Areas, some of which have retained a racially mixed population from the time before their designation came into force owing to failure fully to implement racial homogeneity. While the emergence of grey areas is an expression of black demand or need for housing outside their own designated space, along with willingness on the part of property owners to sell or rent irrespective of racial classification of the potential occupant, it also reflects a growing reluctance of local authorities and the police to monitor who lives where and to prosecute those offending the Group Areas Act.

While grey areas are now to be found in most large cities, Johannesburg has attracted most attention. Pickard-Cambridge (1988, p. vii) comments as follows:

> 'grey areas' arose primarily from a spontaneous and irreversible process in which acute housing shortages in black areas - created by the Group Areas Act itself and by

24

government housing policies which sought to curb African urbanisation by limiting the provision of city houses - forced black people to seek housing in white-designated areas. They were able to find it because changes in the property market had created an accommodation surplus in the white inner cities; property owners and estate agents were thus willing to let property to black people even though this was illegal.

White migration to the suburbs had helped to create available housing in locations much more convenient to blacks than their own, usually peripheral, residential areas. Legal constraints were circumvented by such devices as selling or letting to White nominees acting for blacks. That property owners or their agents would flaunt the law could be explained, at least in part, by the money that could be made by satisfying the pent-up demand by blacks for decent housing in good neighbourhoods. Indeed, the vulnerability of illegal black residence in White areas, as well as scarcity of accommodation, gives scope for exploitation on the part of landlords.

Black people first began moving into Johannesburg's inner city in the mid-1970s. The first were Coloureds and Indians, impelled by a housing shortage exacerbated by evictions from their original inner residential areas to peripheral townships. By 1983 between 8000 and 12,000 blacks were estimated to be living in White inner-city areas. In 1985 a study by J. Fick and C. B. De Coning of the Rand Afrikaans University suggested that 9000 Coloureds, 6500 Indians and 4500 Africans were residing in the Hillbrow, Berea and Joubert Park area on the northern edge of Johannesburg's central business district; 27 per cent of those in 'mixed' apartment blocks in these

areas were not White. The number of Africans joining the Coloured and Indian pioneers indicated an important new development. By 1987 there were claims that half the tenants in rented accommodation in the inner city were black; in 1988 a city newspaper put the figure for people 'of colour' in Hillbrow at some 30,000 (**Star**, 18 May 1988). A survey by the United Building Society in 1989 found 50 per cent of the inhabitants of Hillbrow and 70 per cent of those in Joubert Park to be 'non-white'. Today, the population of the general area affected by the greying process is put at about 100,000.

Hillbrow has developed a distinctive, almost cosmopolitan character, only partly a result of the greying process. Michael Hornsby has described it as: 'a square mile of flats, shops, restaurants, street cafes, bars, nightclubs, strip joints and sleazy hotels, some of them thinly disguised brothels where prostitutes of all shades ply their trade. It aspires to be a Soho or a Greenwich Village, where the strait-laced Calvinist South Africa lets down its hair' (**The Times**, 6 May 1987). This kind of impression, coupled with vibrant street life, association with Johannesburg's 'gay' community, a reputation for high crime, and some signs of apartment blocks becoming overcrowded and dilapidated, creates an image of impropriety and immorality which opponents of grey areas are able to use in defence of strict Group Areas. However, a study of the actual incidence of crime in 1984-86 showed the number of murder, assault and rape cases per 10,000 population in Hillbrow to be lower than in the White suburb of Mondeor (**Weekly Mail**, 24 April - 4 May 1988).

That greying is by no means a straightforward and uniform process is illustrated by the Mayfair district, to the west of central Johannesburg. A study by staff

*'Grey areas' representative of the breakdown of racial residential segregation: **Plate 9** (l) hotel in the (White) Albert Park district of Durban where people not classified as White are living; **Plate 10** (r) Mayfair in Johannesburg, where Indians are buying and improving homes in a White Group Area.*

of the Department of Development Studies at the Rand Afrikaans University has found that about 13,000 Indians have moved into this White area of modest detached and semi-detached housing over the past decade, to make up almost half the total population today. They have generally come from 'middle class' backgrounds, and tend to have better qualifications and higher incomes than the White inhabitants. Mayfair has been upgraded considerably since the influx of Indians, with many of the original houses renovated or even rebuilt. Property values in the area were found to have increased by 161 per cent in the previous four years, compared with only 20 per cent in Johannesburg as a whole (SAIRR, 1989, p. 229).

The Albert Park area on the western fringe of Durban's central business district reproduces some of Hillbrow's characteristics on a smaller scale. It is a White Group Area, comprising blocks of flats and residential hotels. Flats vacated by Whites moving to the suburbs created a vacuum, filled by blacks whose own areas can provide neither as satisfactory accommodation nor as convenient a location. The greying process began discreetly in the 1970s, was noticeable by 1980, and has greatly accelerated since the latter part of 1988. Recent estimates put the black population at about 1000 or 1500 (**Daily News**, 28 March 1989, 13 April 1989); other claims are higher, equivalent to 40 per cent of the area's entire population of 6000 or so.

Further variety is provided by the movement of blacks into White suburban areas beyond the inner city. In Sandton in the northern suburbs of Johannesburg, for example, township unrest in 1985 caused thousands of Africans to move temporarily to the homes of friends already in White areas, or to the suburban White back gardens where domestic servants traditionally have their quarters - and which today reputedly provide homes for thousands of other blacks. Indians are moving into parts of White Westville in Durban, with the assistance of the Westville Residents' Support Group which, like the Central Durban Residents Association in Albert Park, represents practical opposition to Group Areas. Cape Town's grey area of Woodstock, adjoining the site of District Six, has never achieved its proclaimed White status, retaining a substantial Coloured population and attracting others of all race groups who prefer to live in an integrated area.

For a long time, the government refused to recognise the greying process. As recently as 1987 the Deputy Minister of Constitutional Development and planning, P. J. Badenhorst, was quoted as saying, 'The Act doesn't allow open or grey areas ... there is no such thing as a grey area'. However, the growing reality of the local breakdown of the Group Areas Act, along with the tendency in some places simply to turn a blind eye, has precipitated serious reconsideration of the principle of strict racial segregation in South Africa's cities.

It was in commerce rather than residence that the first formal concessions were made. Black businesses, especially those run by Indians, had for years been operating on a modest scale in White areas, through the use of White nominees or front men. While this contravened at least the spirit of the law, some local authorities found no objection to the integration of commercial activity. Early in 1986 the central business districts of Durban and Johannesburg were proclaimed free trading areas for all races, and by the end of the year about 20 other cities had followed. By the end of 1988 it was reported that 90 CBDs had been opened up, including those in some otherwise conservative cities (SAIRR, 1989, p. 341). A few cities were even seeking free trade, and residence, status for the entire municipal area.

Early in the 1980s the government initiated an investigation into the operation of the Group Areas Act. The process proved protracted, and publication of a President's Council report was postponed in 1986 amidst speculation that recommendations accepting existing grey areas and proposing the opening up of others went too far for the government. However, a bill to legalise so-called 'free settlement areas' was eventually brought forward and passed by the (White) House of Assembly in September 1988. The Coloured and Indian Houses refused to approve the legislation on the grounds that the Group Areas Act itself should be repealed to make all residential areas open, but these objections were overridden by the President's Council. The Free Settlement Areas Act was signed by the State President in January 1989.

This Act, and its accompanying Local Government Affairs in Free Settlement Areas Act, make provision for the designation of specific residential areas for occupation by members of any race group, and for non-racial management committees within them. In November 1989 the first four such areas were announced: District Six in Cape Town, Country View midway between Johannesburg and Pretoria, Windmill Park south of Boksburg (east of Johannesburg), and the Warwick Avenue Triangle to the west of Durban city centre. The exclusion (to date) of Hillbrow and other firmly established grey areas raises questions as to how far the government is presently prepared to go. There is also the issue of whether facilities such as schools abandoned by the Whites who have moved out will be made available to others. Some measures proposed to tighten up conformity to the Group Areas Act suggest that the acceptance of free or open areas may merely represent coming to terms with reality, in a way that appears to make concessions to those who wish to live in racially mixed communities while perhaps maintaining strict segregation elsewhere. But the entire concept of Group Areas can no longer survive any serious political dialogue involving blacks.

Petty apartheid

The provisions of the Reservation of Separate Amenities Act of 1953, legalising separate facilities for different race groups, were strictly implemented and enforced over the succeeding two decades. This involved the construction of separate premises, or at least separate entrances or sections, and the erection of signs indicating which group or groups had access. Much of this merely formalised the status quo, but the more conspicuous separation of the races, along with the implementation of the Group Areas Act, served to demarcate geographical space firmly as the province of some people and not others - depending on racial classification.

There has been considerable erosion of petty apartheid in recent years. The first relaxations came in the 1970s, when 'White' facilities were permitted to admit Blacks, Indians and Coloureds by acquiring so-called 'international' status. By the early 1980s there were about 80 'international' hotels and 50 restaurants, along with a few sports facilities such as race courses. However, racial mixing in 'international' facilities was greatly restricted by the very limited basis for inter-racial social contact in everyday life, as well as by the cost of using them which was prohibitive to most blacks. While some token integration was achieved in sport, this again was greatly restricted by residential segregation and the traditional social distance between the races.

Subsequent changes have involved a combination of central government relaxation of the law to enable multi-racial usage of facilities, local government desegregation initiatives, and pressure on the part of individuals and groups opposed to some or all separate amenities. Acts of defiance on the part of blacks have helped to highlight particular aspects of petty apartheid, and to promote a climate more amenable to change. During the 1980s central government buildings gradually lost their segregation signs, and

local authorities, communities and businesses applied successfully to open up a range of facilities for multi-racial use. What developed was, in effect, a system of local options, under which the more progressive local authorities would integrate facility, with others following, but with more conservative places retaining segregation. For example, a few cities opened their libraries to all races in the latter part of the 1970s, while some still reserve them for Whites today. Swimming pools, means of transportation and other facilities in which Whites can come into close physical contact with blacks cause particular difficulty for the racial prejudice of more conservative White people and communities.

The repeal of the Immorality and Prohibition of Mixed Marriages Acts in 1985 was particularly important in a symbolic sense, as well as to those couples attracted to one another across official racial demarcations. These Acts had created extreme distress to some people, though they had not been implemented with great vigour: the Minister of Law and Order reported that while the Immorality Act was in force only 929 people had been arrested, 733 brought to trial and 527 found guilty (SAIRR, 1987, p. 8).

Rather than provide further detail of the step-by-step process of relaxation of petty apartheid, with its variation among both facilities and places, a case study will be used to illustrate the nature of the struggles involved. Beach segregation has been a particularly emotive issue. The gradual breakdown of strict beach segregation, as each coastal town or city has been forced to come to terms with the problem, has revealed not only traditional antipathy of Whites towards blacks but also cultural differences in the way different kinds of people use the amenities of sand, sea and sun. Something of this is reflected in the following depiction of White use of the beach, as compared with that of Africans (Booth and Mbona, 1988, p. 40):

> At the beach the body is a symbol of self-discipline and surveillance. The dominant icons promoted by the leisure industry are the young, attractive and healthy person, and the happy family. The cultural imperative is to look, act and feel in conformity with these images. The 'correct' shape, health and sexuality are critical to the sense of 'normality'. ... Those who want to preserve the beachfront as a site to reinforce white culture portray the black body as threatening the social order. ... African people view the beach as a site of entertainment, as a place to

*Police neglect of crime in black areas is contrasted with the apprehending of blacks on Whites-only beaches (**Cape Times**, 23 Aug. 1989). Adriaan Vlok is Minister of Law and Order.*

unite as a crowd and enjoy social interaction. In a number of respects a visit to the beach is comparable to a medieval carnival; an event celebrated as an ecstatic release from work.

Such differences can be exaggerated, particularly as Blacks increasingly adopt aspects of the lifestyle of Whites (short of seeking a suntan). However, the issue of overcrowding and close physical propinquity raised by beach integration evokes deep White fears of being 'swamped' by Blacks. In this sense South Africa's beaches are an analogy of the wider society.

The desegregation of Durban's beaches serves to illustrate the process in one city. By the 1960s the entire stretch from Durban harbour to beyond the mouth of the Umgeni River had been reserved for Whites, except for three small areas set aside respectively for Africans, Indians and Coloureds (Figure 2.5). The Whites had the beaches onto which the hotels fronted, with the others well away to the north. In 1978 the Amenities Council of Durban City Council recommended that a section of the beachfront be opened to all races, but this provoked such controversy and White opposition that it was four years before Battery Beach Two (at the northern end

of the White stretch) was integrated. Further White beaches were desegregated in 1985, and in 1987 all but two of the remaining racially exclusive beaches were integrated, and renamed as appropriate, to leave South Beach and Addington Beach for Whites only. The significance of the exceptions was that they adjoined an area of hotels patronised largely by conservative Afrikaners on holiday, and there were fears for the city's tourist industry if the preference for Whites-only beaches was no longer satisfied. The opening of these remaining beaches to all races was subsequently rejected a number of times by the City Council; it was finally approved late in 1989.

For the most part, beach integration had been achieved without the inter-racial conflict that opponents had predicted, and 'overcrowding' was confined to particularly busy holiday weekends. National pressure for total desegregation built up through 1989, along with counter exhortations to apprehend those blacks who attempted to use Whites-only beaches. Something of the contorted thinking encouraged by this aspect of petty apartheid is reflected in a statement by Councilor J. Venter, chairman of the city's Management Committee, that: 'The Durban City Council was an equal opportunity

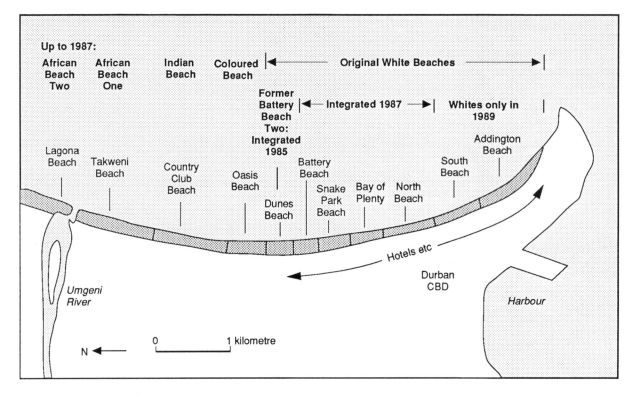

Figure 2.5   Beach segregation and desegregation in Durban
Source: **Indicator South Africa**, 3 (3), 1986, p. 2, updated.

employer and it would not employ only white beach inspectors for whites-only beaches' (**The Natal Mercury**, 25 Aug. 1989). Equal opportunity applied to the implementation of unequal access to the beach.

However, the national tide of opinion was now moving against beach segregation. Earlier in 1989 the renowned author F. A. Venter had asked, in the Afrikaans newspaper **Die Burger**, 'How can a Christian reconcile with his conscience the fact that a white minority prescribes to a majority of his country's citizens and say that they may not swim in the Lord's sea ?', and this seemed more to catch the

spirit of the times than did the traditionally segregationist attitudes of the Afrikaner people. In November 1989, barely two months after taking up the office of State President, F. W. de Klerk announced that the time to repeal the Separate Amenities Act had come, though with careful consideration to the implications. Action on beaches was required without delay, he said, and all beaches would henceforth be accessible to all members of the public. Local authorities were requested to act in the spirit of this decision, insofar as local ordinances and by-laws are concerned.

They are getting there, with the relaxation of petty apartheid: **Plate 11** *(l) signs in Zulu as well as English and Afrikaans show that Durban sea-front is now recognised as a place for Africans;* **Plate 12** *(r) segregation sign on the last Whites-only beaches in Durban in September 1989, shortly before they were integrated.*

Against these trends towards desegregation of facilities has been the reintroduction of petty apartheid in some places. In October 1988 the Conservative Party took control of more than 90 White local authorities, mainly in the Transvaal, and a few councils immediately voted to resegregate certain of their 'public' services. The most notorious case was Boksburg, where the lake, municipal halls, swimming pools and some other facilities were closed to blacks; this elicited a black boycott of White businesses, which caused substantial loss of trade. By the end of 1988 some resegregation had also been introduced in seven other Conservative-controlled towns in the Transvaal. In at least nine other towns it was not necessary to reintroduce segregation, as municipal facilities had never been opened to all races (SAIRR, 1989, p. 28). There continues to be a struggle between these councils, local business suffering from boycotts, general black anger, and central government upset at these conspicuous reversals of its 'reform' of apartheid.

As further evidence of the relaxation (or otherwise) of racial segregation unfolds, it is as well to bear in mind that, in the 1989 general election, almost one-third of the Whites who voted supported the Conservative Party, whose platform included opposition to 'open' residential areas, and whose local activities have demonstrated a willingness to put blacks back in their place. F. Hartzenberg, deputy chairman on the Conservative Party, has been quoted as saying (SAIRR, 1988, p. 1): 'We would not allow a black man to live just anywhere in South Africa'.

Pg 14

3 EXPLAINING APARTHEID

The point has now been reached to step back from the details of how racial separation has been achieved, or otherwise, and to begin to explain what is behind apartheid. Media coverage of South Africa tends to focus selectively on such dramatic events as 'rebel' sports tours, township unrest, police brutality and political prisoners, and this encourages a superficial and unduly narrow interpretation. Apartheid cannot be explained simply as race discrimination arising from antipathy between blacks and Whites. South Africa itself cannot be dismissed simply as a repressive police state. The South African government has, over the years, operated with far more sophistication than is often supposed, and to a more complex purpose than simply keeping races apart or the blacks in their place.

Four interpretations of apartheid will be considered briefly in this chapter. These are: (1) the traditional government perspective of 'separate development', (2) an explanation which emphasises racial domination in the political sphere, (3) one which sees economic exploitation of blacks as the key to apartheid, and (4) a reconsideration which recognises moves towards the selective incorporation of blacks within mainstream South African society. These interpretations are not mutually exclusive nor do they cover all possible views, but they are broadly representative of alternative perspectives. The order in which they appear reflects a changing understanding of apartheid with changing circumstances.

This chapter is designed to provide a bridge between the detail of the first two chapters and the two that follow, in which certain crucial aspects of the structure and restructuring of apartheid introduced here will be considered more fully.

Separate development

The traditional rationale for apartheid propagated by the National Party saw territorial and social separation as the only way of preserving inter-racial harmony and the cultural integrity of each group in a complex 'pluralistic' society. It was thus in the interests of all races, not just to the advantage of Whites. The term 'apartheid' subsequently became so pejorative as no longer to be part of the official lexicon, and was replaced some years ago by 'separate development' and more recently by 'multinational development'. The 1980s saw more emphasis in government pronouncements on cooperation between the races and on their interdependence in the development process. For example, South Africa's official **Yearbook** (RSA, 1983, p. 195) referred to 'a comprehensive programme designed to do justice to all the peoples of South Africa, providing as it does for economic cooperation and interdependence between Black and White, coupled with the highest possible degree of political freedom and self-determination for all in the peculiar circumstances of the country'.

Despite changes in terminology and emphasis, government policy at the national scale remained committed (in public at least) to the Homelands or Bantustans, in their guise as 'self-governing states' or 'independent republics'. The policy as traditionally espoused is explained as follows in a book **Homelands**, issued by the government-sponsored Bantu Investment Corporation (1979, p. 1):

> Since it is the policy of the White government that the Black nations for which it still acts as guardian should eventually be able to exercise the right to full national independence, it is evident that the final geopolitical division of the Republic of South Africa lies at some point in the future. The progressive political development of the Republic's Black peoples and their gradual crystallisation into independent nation states (like their independent Black neighbours in Lesotho, Botswana and Swaziland) will obviously demand an adjustment of the current geopolitical borders and boundaries of the Republic of South Africa. Once the process of emancipation has reached its conclusion, the Republic of South Africa will become a sovereign independent White nation state which will be associated with its Black neighbour states on the basis of political independence and economic interdependence.

Thus would emerge what was sometimes referred to in official circles as a 'constellation of states', in each of which the people would be free to preserve their own ways of life and determine their own destinies.

With Blacks having their own independent states, the question of their political rights within 'White' South Africa would no longer arise. They would be citizens of their own states, with normal responsibilities and rights, including the vote. Within the 'White' Republic, residential separation, often by tribe as well as on the basis of being classified as Black, would encourage those not actually in their Homeland to identify with it. Segregation at the local scale would also assist the Whites, Coloureds and Asians to preserve their own group identities, including the racial purity which is so highly valued by Afrikaners.

The past decade has seen some significant reorientation of the Homeland policy, as theory has confronted reality. Four 'independent' states have been created, but others have resisted. The granting of 'republic' status to KwaNdebele, expected in December 1986, was postponed, and the official position now is that: 'None of the remaining six self-governing territories will be coerced into accepting independence' (RSA, 1989, p. 192). There is even talk of some of the four seeking to have their 'independence' reversed, with reincorporation into the Republic of South Africa the eventual objective.

The basic problem with the Homeland policy of separate development, viewed in its own terms, has been the failure to create either the reality or the appearance of viable independent states. This was recognised in 1980 when the then Prime Minister P. W. Botha stated that it would be impossible to consolidate the land area of each territory in such a way that it would be viable by itself or provide a livelihood for its entire population: 'In most of these territories less than 20 per cent of the population derive their income from their geographic area, and we simply cannot hand over the entire RSA merely to establish viable Black states', he conceded (RSA, 1989, p. 178). New strategies for accelerated economic development were seen as the solution.

Ten years on, the Homelands are still heavily dependent on external sources for their revenue. Table 3.1 shows that the proportion coming from internal sources is as low as 13.9 per cent in KwaNdebele and is rarely much more than a quarter; only in Transkei is the figure more than half. And even these may be substantial overestimates; others put the figures for the TBVC states as only 24 percent for Transkei, 23 for Bophuthatswana, 12 for Venda and 10 for Ciskei, if all central government transfer payments are excluded (SAIRR, 1989, p. 61). The table emphasises the reliance on central (Republic of South Africa) government resources.

The experience of individual Homelands hardly encourages a view of economically viable independent states, as is illustrated by Ciskei, for example. While Ciskei has acquired various trappings of a sovereign nation state, at considerable expense

Table 3.1   **Sources of Homeland revenue for the financial year 1988/89 (R million)**

Homeland	Central government	Loans	Internal revenue	Total	% from internal
Bophuthatswana	403	148	188	738	25.5
Ciskei	910	-	191	1101	17.3
Transkei	660	-	936	1596	58.6
Venda	282	71	194	547	35.5
Gazankulu	408	47	153	608	25.2
KaNgwane	215	30	49	294	16.3
KwaNdebele	208	45	41	294	13.9
KwaZulu	1463	118	387	1968	19.7
Lebowa	860	66	221	1147	19.3
QwaQwa	160	26	120	306	39.2

Source: SAIRR (1989, p. 61), from Homeland estimates. Note that the Homelands generally include various transfer payments from the central (RSA) government under internal revenue, so the proportion from internal sources is likely to be an underestimate.

(see Chapter 2), its attempts to marshal free enterprise behind economic development have not succeeded. B. Streek (in Van der Kooy, 1988, pp. 59-60) explains:

> The reality of development for the million or so people living within the borders of Ciskei is that life has stagnated, and economically speaking, has almost certainly deteriorated during the first five years of independence. ... Whatever estimation is used, the household incomes in the rural areas as well as those in the more remote urban areas, are incredibly low: the vast majority of people are, in anyone's terms, very poor.

And the one-third of Ciskei's population living in large urban areas like Mdantsane and Zwelitshe, themselves little more than suburban extensions of the city of East London across the border in the RSA, depend greatly on employment in the Republic. The main concentration of industrial development in Ciskei, at Dimbaza, owes its existence to the 'decentralisation' of activity from the Republic (see Chapter 5).

If the economy of the Homelands raises questions as to the success of separate development, their political practice has been no more encouraging. For example, the Ciskei government was until recently highly centralised around Life President Lenox Sebe, leader of the only legal political party in the Homeland; he had five homes, reported to have cost R4.4 million (Van der Kooy, 1988, p. 63). Sebe's power base remained rooted in the traditional chiefs and tribal authorities. His government was frequently portrayed as inefficient as well as undemocratic, corrupt and repressive. Sebe was overthrown by a coup in March 1990.

Ciskei may to some extent be an extreme case. However, in most respects it typifies the Homelands, 'independent' or otherwise, as artificial creations of the Republic of South Africa, with some symbols and semblance of national identity but no serious prospect of economic viability. The original conception of separate development and the creation of independent Black nation states, already evidently compromised, seems likely to become even more muted in official strategy statements, as the government is forced to reconsider the entire logic of its national-scale policy which lacks legitimacy to large proportions of the Black majority population.

The fact that apartheid as separate development has foundered is by no means surprising. The idea of spatial separation as a means of preserving cultural integrity rested on insecure moral as well as practical foundations from the start, giving a veneer of legitimacy to the prejudice with which Whites tended to regarded members of other races. The Afrikaners in particular had developed a culture of racial superiority, sharpened in their violent historical struggle with Africans for land, and for a long time given religious justification by their Dutch Reformed Church. The policy of separate development to some extent reflected the paternalist view that the Whites had a mission to Christianise and educate an inferior people, their own civilised standards and institutions providing models to which Blacks should aspire.

But the strategy went further than simply indulging the sense of superiority of one group of people towards others and their way of life. Apartheid as separate development also involved racism, in the sense of attempts by a dominant group to use racial ascriptions and thinking to exclude a subordinate group from the material benefits, status or power that they might otherwise have enjoyed. The legal structure created to implement apartheid, including tribal Homelands and race Group Areas, is therefore a case of institutionalised racism. And the elevated ideals of separate development can, for the most part, be reduced to more mundane objectives of political domination and economic exploitation.

Political domination

The official rationale for the policy of apartheid as separate development has for long been challenged by those who view it as a faintly disguised strategy for the perpetuation of racial domination. The geographical transfer of Black citizenship and political rights (eg the franchise) from 'White' South Africa to the Homelands would restore White numerical supremacy in the RSA, with more people than the two remaining groups (Coloureds and Asians) together (see Table 1.1). Instead of emancipating the Blacks and giving them true political independence, separate development simply keeps them in a position of peripheral subordination to the Whites. The allocation of the Blacks to ten separate Homelands may be interpreted as a strategy for divide and rule, rather than as a means of preserving tribal integrity as the official government line sometimes asserts.

That territorial disaggregation is an important feature of separate development, as political domination is illustrated by the Homeland 'consolidation' process, which the government has yet to finalise. Not only are there ten different Homelands, but most of them comprise a number of separate blocks of land. KwaZulu, the most populous, remains highly fragmented and will still have ten blocks separated by 'White' land if the consolidation plan is ever completed. The 'independent republic' of Bophuthatswana has six separate blocks, one of them (Thaba 'Nchu) more than 300km from its nearest neighbouring block.

In addition to this 'Balkanisation', the boundaries have been drawn so as to exclude from the Homelands most industrial centres of any importance, most mineral resources, and practically all transportation lines. All but the smallest White settlements have also been excluded, the incorporation into Bophuthatswana of the town of Mafeking, renamed Mafikeng, being an exception. The Homelands have no ports, and only limited access to the coasts. In short, it is difficult to see how these areas, even after consolidation, could ever have been viewed by the South African government as providing a satisfactory geographical basis for economically viable and truly independent nation states of the kind to which the contemporary world has become accustomed. Thus the credibility of the official rationale is called into question; political domination is a far more plausible explanation for the Homeland policy. It is therefore hardly surprising that those four deemed to be 'independent' have failed to achieve external recognition.

Further support for the political domination interpretation is provided by population figures. The discussion around Table 2.2 in the previous chapter has already drawn attention to the large numbers of Blacks outside their tribal Homeland. Census figures for 1980, before the exclusion of the TBVC area, enabled a distinction to be made between the so-called 'de facto' and 'de jure' populations of the ten Homelands. De facto refers to those actually there, de jure to the tribal population allocated to the Homeland in question. The de jure Homeland population was less than the de facto population by the number of people of other tribal groups in the Homeland in question; this was generally fairly small but exceeded 400,000 in the case of Bophuthatswana (ie one-third of the actual population were non-Tswana) and almost 300,000 for Lebowa. More significant, however, was the difference between the de jure population and the total for that tribal group: the proportion of the tribal total actually resident in their Homeland varied from about 60 per cent in the case of three of the four 'independent republics' (the exception was Venda) to as low as 16

per cent of the South African Swazi living in KaNgwane and 11 per cent of the Sotho in QwaQwa. Of the total of about 20 million Blacks, just less than half actually lived in their supposed Homeland. Estimates for 1988 (from Tables 1.1 and 2.2) show almost 27 million Blacks in greater South Africa with 13.8 million in the ten Homelands, leaving over 13 million somewhere else, presumably in 'White' South Africa. This figure, along with those living in the wrong Homeland, is an indication of the discrepancy between the theory of tribal Homelands or Black states and the reality of the actual population distribution.

Within the cities, the racial domination interpretation emphasises the fact that the implementation of the Group Area Act has generally favoured the Whites. They have gained some attractive and conveniently located residential areas from the Coloureds and Indians, who have been forced into peripheral areas (see above, Figures 2.2 and 2.3), where they pose less competition or threat to White control of the inner city. There is an analogy here with the assignment of the Blacks to peripheral locations nationally: the detached tribal Homeland blocks fragment what would otherwise be a continuous crescent of Black territory threatening the economic heartland of the Witwatersrand centred on Johannesburg.

During the 1980s the legitimacy of the Homelands strategy as a device to externalise Black political rights came increasingly into question. The government has itself been forced to change position; as its official **Yearbook** puts it (RSA, 1989, p. 189):

> Until fairly recently it was government policy that all Black communities outside the self-governing territories and TBVC states should satisfy their political aspirations beyond local government level through the institutions of the various territories. ... By the early 1980s it was clear that the time had come for a reappraisal of the policies in relation to the Blacks outside these territories, especially the urbanised communities which included people who were born there and had never seen their ethno-cultural territory.

The flow of Blacks to the cities, despite 'influx control', was a major stimulus to change in government policy with respect to urbanisation, regional development and administration at the sub-national scale (considered in Chapter 5).

The main political outcome has been a reversal of

policy on citizenship. With the 'independence' of the TBVC territories, all people deemed to be their citizens ceased to be citizens of the Republic of South Africa. Citizenship of these territories was determined largely by language and ethnic descent, and 8-9 million previously South African citizens became aliens in South African law. The logical extension would have been to deprive people of the other six Homelands of their South African citizenship, on the grounds that they should exercise their political rights, including the vote, in their own 'self-governing' territory. However, in 1985 the State President announced that all Blacks living in these territories, or resident elsewhere but associated with them by kinship or culture (ie tribe), would remain South African citizens, even if their particular territory should become independent. In 1986 the Restoration of South African Citizenship Act made provision for TBVC citizens who qualified by birth or length of residence in the RSA to regain South African citizenship, while retaining that of their own 'independent' state. While this was estimated to affect only about 1.75 million TBVC citizens, this Act, along with the 1985 measure, put an end to any remaining expectations that Blacks could be denied a political role in the Republic of South Africa through the Homeland strategy.

Economic exploitation

The political domination interpretation, like simplistic critiques stressing discrimination, tends to portray apartheid largely if not exclusively in racial terms. In this respect it resembles the traditional rationale for separate development, with its emphasis on the preservation of cultural (or racial) integrity and the elimination of inter-group (ie race) conflict. However, there is another interpretation, which sees racial domination as part of a broader system which has an economic purpose: that of facilitating the exploitation of cheap (Black) labour. This interpretation also argues that although racial conflict is an important element in South Africa, an exclusively racial interpretation of apartheid obscures the class affiliations and cleavages which are present in any capitalist society and which can transcend racial identity.

There are two important ways in which the policy of apartheid, in its classical form as separate development, can reduce the cost of labour in South Africa. First, the Homelands help to diffuse Black political power, thus damping down pressure for higher wages, better working conditions, fringe benefits and social services, which can be exerted by an organised and united working class. The stress on racial and tribal affiliation under apartheid constrains the development of a broader working-class consciousness. Discriminatory legislation, whereby certain jobs were until recently reserved for Whites, other races are paid less than Whites, and trade union activities on the part of Blacks are restricted, all uses racial identity to keep down the cost of certain people's labour.

The second way in which labour costs can be depressed is that the Homelands enable part of them to be externalised, in a literal geographical sense, as far as 'White' South Africa is concerned, just as political right can be transferred. This is because certain of these costs are borne within the Homelands, or even outside South Africa itself. This strategy has been used to particular effect with the migrant labour on which the mines have traditionally relied (see next chapter). All the employers need pay for the migrant worker is the cost of keeping the individual alive, fit and reasonably content during the contract period; wages little above subsistence are often enough to attract this kind of labour. Migrant workers remit or bring back money to the Homeland for the support of their families but this is supplemented from the local agricultural sector. When at home 'resting' or unemployed between contracts, migrants are supported by the local economy. Thus part of the full cost of maintaining a migrant labour system is externalised or transferred to the areas of origin: the Homelands and states bordering South Africa.

Some of the costs associated with what is, in effect, a permanent Black workforce in 'White' South Africa are also externalised, through the requirement that certain social services be provided in the Homelands for their citizens in the 'White' Republic. Where Black dormitory towns on the edge of 'White' cities are defined as part of a Homeland, Blacks working in 'White' South Africa as so-called 'frontier commuters' (see next chapter) have their social welfare costs met in the Homeland. Thus 'White' South Africa avoids part of the full cost of the labour which it needs, and business profits accordingly.

The political 'independence' of some of the Homelands makes it easier for the South African government to argue that the social support of those who live there is the responsibility of the governments of those Black 'states' and not that of 'White' South Africa, even if large numbers of their citizens actually work in the White city. In this sense the South African government's position can be portrayed as perfectly normal, just as it is with respect to denying the franchise to citizens of supposedly foreign independent states.

Ciskei may, again, be used as a case in point. In 1988 there were almost 14,000 migrant workers from Ciskei employed in the mines of South Africa; the addition of other migrants and frontier commuters would take the figure of those working beyond the Homeland borders to over 100,000, or somewhat more than half Ciskei's labour force. The situation has been elaborated by Cadman (1986, p. 10) as follows:

> The large scale export of labour from the Ciskei has extensive ramifications for the area. The influx control system ensures that the homeland bears the responsibility for housing, educating and supporting the family of the migrant or commuter, while the South African economy reaps the benefits of the workers' labour. In addition, the Ciskei serves as a 'dumping ground' for the old, disabled and unemployed. The South African fiscus does, however, make a considerable contribution to the provision of the above services.

Over 80 per cent of Ciskei's revenue comes from the RSA government (Table 3.1), as what might be regarded an investment in one of its labour reserves. That South Africa can portray this as 'foreign aid' is a further aspect of the ingenious applied geography of apartheid.

Figure 3.1 summarises the argument, in a simplified sketch of the main features of the spatial structure of exploitation in South Africa. The country is portrayed

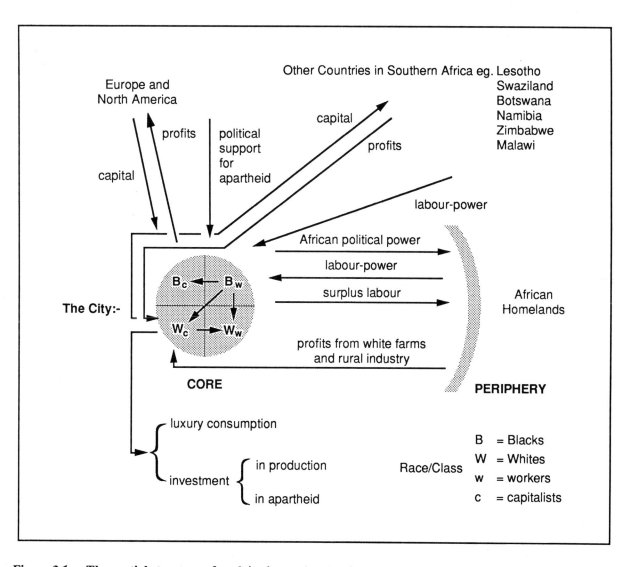

Figure 3.1   The spatial structure of exploitation under classical apartheid
Source: Smith (1977, p. 262).

*Recruiting Blacks into the consumer society is the objective of much advertising: **Plate 13** (l) in Soweto, dominating early township housing; **Plate 14** (r) in Mabopane, a township in Bophuthatswana.*

as a simple core/periphery dichotomy, the core representing the city and the periphery the Homelands. The periphery provides cheap labour (some of which also comes from other countries in southern Africa) and acts as a repository for surplus labour as well as for the transfer of political power from the core. Profits are generated and capital accumulated in the city, from the exploitation of cheap labour. A process of income redistribution in the core is suggested, whereby the product of Black labour benefits White capital owners or businesses (promoting luxury consumption, investment in new productive capacity and expenditure required to maintain apartheid). The White working class gains from protected employment and the artificial maintenance of high living standards, and a small Black capitalist class themselves gain from the availability of cheap labour. Profits made in South Africa by multinational corporations are repatriated to Europe and North America, in return for which comes political support (or muted opposition) for the South African government. Some capital generated in South Africa is also invested elsewhere in the sub-continent, as adjoining or nearby states which might otherwise be hostile (eg Zimbabwe) become tied to South Africa by economic dependence.

This interpretation of apartheid stresses the economic foundations of South African society. It incorporates something of the racial political domination perspective, setting this in a broader context. While stressing that apartheid and capitalism in South Africa are mutually supportive, it does recognise some contradictions between them. For example, racial domination cuts labour costs but reduces the mobility of Black labour and in some respects impedes its efficient utilisation. Low Black wages limit purchasing power, which acts as a constraint on economic growth, and the cost of maintaining

apartheid (including subsidy of Homeland budgets) depresses White living standards .

The extent to which apartheid is functional to the needs of capitalism is the subject of continuing debate (eg Lipton, 1985; Stadler, 1987; Tomlinson and Addleson, 1987; Wolpe, 1988; Nattrass, 1989). Despite a decline in recent years, the rate of profit in South Africa remains high compared with other advanced capitalist countries. However, major corporations are often severe critics of government, claiming that the rigidities of racial discrimination interfere with market forces and that the sanctions imposed by other countries in response to apartheid impede economic progress. The withdrawal of some large firms from South Africa in the second half of the 1980s called into question the extent to which the White government and international capital continue to share common interests. Business is concerned about the Nationalists' capacity to maintain the social stability on which reliable profit-making depends, and has also to consider image problems arising from association with apartheid. If fundamental reform takes place, or even if social control can be maintained under White domination conveyed in more acceptable terms, the support of international capital may well be regained - as long as Black labour remains relatively cheap.

Selective incorporation

South African economy, society and polity has changed in some important respects in recent years, and this has required modification of existing interpretations. Soon after his election as Prime Minister in 1978, P. W. Botha was telling the Whites that they must 'adapt or die' and that 'apartheid is a recipe for permanent conflict'. That apartheid itself has officially been declared dead was pointed out at the start of the first chapter. This did not, however, mean that the original principle of racial separation had been abandoned - far from it. There has certainly been a significant relaxation of petty apartheid, and some formal concessions on strict residential segregation with the introduction of Free Settlement Areas. And the 1984 constitution represented a retreat from total White monopoly of political power. But the basic policy instruments of Homelands and Group Areas remain virtually intact in early 1990, as does the racially divided tri-cameral parliament. Aspects of apartheid have thus been restructured, but with the government responding to pressure and necessity rather than taking a positive lead. Nationalist thinking remains wedded to 'groups', ie it is still racial in origin if not always in the manner of its expression.

However, there are pointers towards more fundamental change, evident well before F. W. de Klerk assumed the office of State President in 1989 with unusually reformist rhetoric and the promise to release Nelson Mandela. The details are reserved for the next two chapters, but they hinge on the final abandonment of a principle which was accepted in government circles virtually without question until the late 1970s: that Blacks outside their traditional territories are in White South Africa merely as 'temporary sojourners' (in the customary phrase), there just as long as their labour is needed. It has been clearly accepted for some time that Blacks in large numbers are a permanent feature of the Republic's population, especially in the major cities, and that some racial integration is an inevitable consequence. Furthermore, Blacks in growing numbers are adopting the consumption patterns and culture of the Whites, as economic advances enable some of them them to afford 'middle class' lifestyles.

Yet for some of the Nationalists, and presumably all those one-third of White voters who supported the Conservatives in 1989, continued White rule is non-negotiable and one-person-one-vote inconceivable. In so far as the pace of change may be within the control of the Whites, the problem faced by government is how to incorporate some if not all of the Blacks into the institutions and society of the Republic, while not losing control to the extent of threatening the interests of the White group. Dr F. van Zyl Slabbert, former leader of the opposition Progressive Federal Party (**Financial Mail,** 29 Aug. 1986), has commented as follows:

> The government has accepted that it cannot separate away those who are not white from its own position of domination. Now it seeks ways to integrate them without losing its position of domination. Before, it tried for separation and white domination, now it tries for integration and white domination. ... government at first wanted to create a multi-cultural society through separation; it is now prepared to create a multi-racial society through integration. ... it first tried to exclude and divide and rule; now it is prepared to include and divide and rule.

The process of inclusion relates not only to the formal position of the Blacks as well as Coloureds and Indians, within new political institutions, but also to the co-optation of a compliant middle class from members of these groups as buffer against more radical change. One intention of recent reforms has been, 'to replace racial criteria with market principles in determining access to opportunities within the capitalist social order' (Stadler, 1987, p. 2). Thus class affiliation may increasingly divide blacks, frustrating a common political purpose in challenging

*Selective incorporation in Black housing: **Plate 15** (l) dormitories providing primitive family accommodation in the Cape Town township of Langa; **Plate 16** (r) new private housing opportunities in Khayelitsha, for those few who can afford it.*

White control. And a class alliance with well-to-do blacks could be part of the Whites' survival strategy in a post-apartheid South Africa.

The crucial question over the past few years has been whether the government has the time required for its own form of social and political reconstruction. Its reforms have done little if anything to satisfy mass Black aspirations, and a White right-wing backlash is evident in the rise of the Conservative Party and the emergence of the neo-fascist organisations such as the Afrikaans Resistance Movement. The general election (for Whites) called in 1987 was seen as a necessary test of support for Botha's strategy of limited reforms and a tough stance on internal dissent. Since then, external pressure has continued, in the form of sanctions and disinvestment. And now the ANC has become an increasingly potent force for changes possibly more radical than many liberal opponents of apartheid can contemplate, far less endorse. At the time of writing, well into 1990, it is still too early to see how the de Klerk government plans to negotiate Blacks into the political process at the national level. Meanwhile, Blacks are continuing to incorporate themselves, into the political life of South Africa as well as its economy, and increasingly on their own terms.

- quotes

- when discussing Regional Geography, particularly in the area of South Africa, may attack the subject focussing on one of many different topics.

- could discuss ...

- will talk about: 'people of SA

2 racial separation; inequality

3 Population Removals

4

5 S.A. under Democracy

overwhelmingly controversial

39

4 ECONOMY AND LABOUR

'They are only supplying a commodity, the commodity of labour. ... it is labour we are importing and not labourers as individuals.'
(Nationalist member of parliament, 1960s)

This chapter considers in more detail the relationship between economic activity, population, and the way in which people participate in the economy to earn a living. South Africa is a capitalist society: the means of production are privately owned, for the most part (despite substantial state involvement in certain strategic sectors), with the mass of the people selling their labour to private business or public service. In this sense, the country shares familiar characteristics of other 'western' market economies. What is distinctive about South Africa is the way in which its economy, society and political system has been structured and restructured, with substantial involvement on the part of the state, so as to take advantage of cheap black labour. And apartheid has been central to this process. The outcome has implications not only for the economic role of black people, and in particular Africans, as often little more than the commodity of labour, but also for their struggle to make a living in a society organised systematically to exclude them from many of its benefits while requiring them to carry a disproportionately large share of some of its burdens.

Economic structure

The development of an advanced industrial economy in South Africa was closely associated with the exploitation of minerals, most spectacularly gold and diamonds. The country's mineral wealth is extensive and varied, and includes material of great strategic importance as well as essential elements in modern manufacturing. It was its minerals which first brought substantial numbers of European settlers inland, especially to the Transvaal with its sparse population of White farmers who had successfully contested the Africans for land. And it was the needs of the rapidly growing mining industry which prompted resolutions to the problem of labour supply which still strongly influence social and racial relationships today.

Mining provides employment for about three-quarters of a million people. But it is their strategic significance which give the mines such an important position in the South African economy. The outside world in general and the 'western' capitalist world in particular depends on South Africa for crucial minerals, and this acts as a constraint on American and European political opposition. For example, the United States obtains 61 per cent of its chromium imports from South Africa, 53 per cent of vanadium and industrial diamonds, 42 per cent of platinum group metals, and a high proportion of imports of some other minerals critical to military operations. Table 4.1 shows South Africa's contribution to production and reserves of major minerals for which the country is ranked first or second in output within the 'western' world.

Conspicuous by its absence is oil. South Africa's lack of a domestic source of oil is a major weakness in the face of threats of sanctions - hence the strategic significance of the Sasolberg plant south of Johannesburg, built in 1955 to produce oil from the plentiful national coal resources, and the larger facilities set up in 1975-76 to the east near Secunda. The country's crucial oil infrastructure is completed by harbour facilities for imports and refining (sanctions notwithstanding), pipelines, and storage units in the Transvaal industrial areas.

Gold remains vitally important to the South African economy, making it highly sensitive to volatile international markets. A rise in the price of gold stimulates the economy, by encouraging investment in the gold mining industry and through the multiplier effect on other activities; a fall in price can induce or exacerbate recession, as in the early 1980s. The role of gold in the international monetary system is a further element in the strategic important of South Africa, giving the capitalist world a strong vested interest in both the political stability of the country and perpetuation of the cheap labour on which the low production cost of gold depends.

However, minerals are far less important in the economy than they used to be. The role of agriculture, which played a prominent part in the country's economic history, has also been substantially reduced. Table 4.2 summarises changes in the origin of GDP, revealing the growing importance of manufacturing, utilities and other services.

Before going further into the economic structure of South Africa it is necessary to mention the problem of measurement. Just as population figures are liable to error, so it is with economic activity - the more so

Table 4.1   South Africa's role in selected world mineral production and reserves

Mineral	Production 1985 (per cent)		Reserves 1986 (per cent)	
	World	'West'	World	'West'
Alumino-silicates	39	48	38	47
Antimony	14	23	3	6
Chrome	32	49	55	58
Coal	5	11	11	20
Ferrochromium	26	37		
Ferromanganese	9	14		
Fluorspar	7	13	10	30
Gold	43	55	48	60
Manganese metal	54	60		
Manganese ore	15	28	79	92
Platinum group metals	23	43	70	83
Uranium		14		15
Vanadium	43	76	33	50
Vermiculite	35	37		40
Zirconium minerals	20	23	18	21

Source: RSA (1989, pp. 314, 319). The 'West' is the world excluding the USSR, Eastern Europe, China, Cuba, Kampuchea, North Korea, Laos, Mongolia and Vietnam. South Africa excludes the TBVC area. Gaps indicate no data.

Table 4.2   Sectoral origin of Gross Domestic Product 1911-1987 (per cent)

Sector	1911	1939	1987
Gold mining	18.7	16.3	8.8
Other mining	8.9	2.0	4.8
Agriculture, forestry and fishing	21.1	13.6	5.7
Manufacturing, construction, electricity, gas, water	5.5	16.6	30.7
Other services	45.8	51.5	50.0

Source: RSA (1989, p. 398).

when the African people are concerned. The regulation imposed by apartheid society is such that the act of settling and trying to make a living in some places is illegal, and those concerned understandably attempt to avoid official scrutiny. There is also the existence of a growing 'informal sector' to the economy, involving large numbers of Africans (see later in this chapter), which by its very nature is largely unrecorded in official statistics. Added to this is the increasing difficulty in obtaining data for the TBVC area comparable to those for the RSA, as the South African government has taken their 'independence' to the logical conclusion of leaving them out of its national economic accounting. The consequence of all this is that figures for employment

and output in South Africa are liable to error, and usually substantially on the low side of the 'true' figures.

Subject to this reservation, Table 4.3 summarises the employment structure of the RSA (ie excluding Transkei, Bophuthatswana, Venda and Ciskei) by race groups. The total is roughly one-third of the Republic's population. If those economically active in the TBVC area are the same proportion of their population a further 2 million or so would be added. But higher unemployment in the TBVC area reduces the actual figure, perhaps to 1.5 million, which would give a total of somewhat over 12 million in greater South Africa, about two-thirds of them Black.

Table 4.3   Employment structure by race group (1000s)

Category	Blacks	Whites	Coloureds	Asians	Total
Economically active population 1988	7,090	2,019	1,208	340	10,657
Employed in urban areas (per cent) 1986 *	39.6	89.6	77.8	93.4	55.9
Employed in mining 1987	669	81	9	1	760
Employed in private manufacturing 1988	712	393	45	389	1,339
Employed in public sector 1988	860	659	199	40	1,758

Source: SAIRR (1988, p. 335; 1989, pp. 395-7); * from Central Statistical Service, RSA.

However, a smaller proportion of economically active Blacks work in urban areas than is the case with the other race groups.

Blacks dominate mining, and account for just over half the manufacturing employment in the RSA (a proportion of which has remained much the same for the past half century). They are not quite as well represented in the public sector. Asians are heavily involved in manufacturing, far less so in the public sector, whereas the Coloureds have more jobs in services than manufacturing and even more in agriculture.

About 5 million of those economically active are reported to be in agriculture and domestic service. However, figures for these activities are even more difficult to establish than in other sectors, as the conditions under which Blacks are employed by farmers and households are often casual and traditional agricultural practices in the Homelands make it hard to define who is actually 'economically active'. Earnings in agriculture and domestic service are generally much lower than in other sectors; for example farm workers averaged only R103 per month in 1986 (SAIRR, 1989, p. 429). The large number of people involved helps to explain the low living standards among the mass of the Black population.

Economic geography

The economy of South Africa is highly polarised geographically. In the early stages, economic activity was concentrated in the coastal enclaves of Cape Town and, later, Durban, after the typical pattern of colonial development elsewhere. The discovery of gold shifted the economic centre of gravity inland, to the Witwatersrand, the supremacy of which was later consolidated by industrialisation. The major coastal cities of the pre-mining era survived and prospered as ports, funnelling goods to and from the interior.

The spatial structure of the modern economy is shown in Figure 4.1. The pattern is dominated by the principal metropolitan agglomeration centred on Johannesburg, usually referred to as the PWV region (Pretoria, Witwatersrand, Vereeniging). This is part of a wider area of relatively intensive economic activity which continues along the main communications corridor to Durban. Other areas of relatively intensive development (the 'inner periphery') correspond with the inland cities of Kimberley and Bloemfontein and extend along much of the south coast. Areas of less intensive activity (the 'intermediate periphery') come next, then the 'outer periphery' of largely agricultural areas. The Homelands form part of this outer periphery, ringing the economic heartland centred on the PWV region.

Almost 70 per cent of South Africa's GDP is generated in the eight main metropolitan centres. The PWV region alone accounts for 40 per cent. The rest of 'White' South Africa generates about 30 per cent. The Homelands (including the 'independent republics') account for only about 5 per cent of GDP. These figures are in sharp contrast to the distribution of population, which divides roughly into about one-third in the major metropolitan centres, a quarter in the rest of 'White' South Africa and two-fifths in the Homelands.

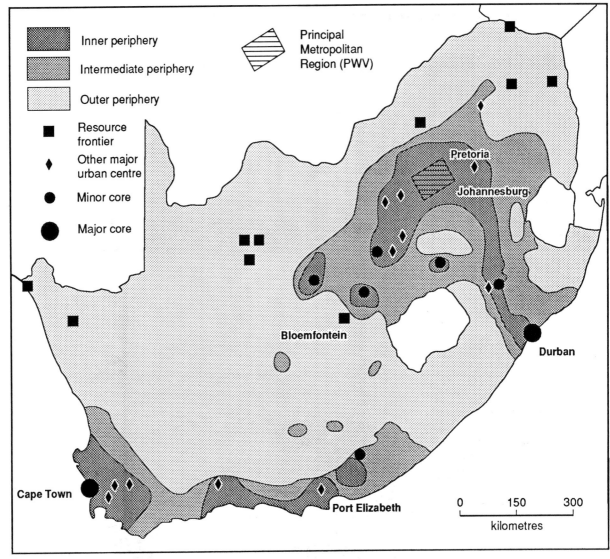

Figure 4.1   The spatial structure of the South African economy
Source: based on Fair (1982, p. 51) after J. Browett; for Homelands see Figure 1.1.

That this geographical concentration of production has increased in recent years is indicated in Table 4.4. A division into three broad areas shows the metropolitan core having increased its share of production (ie GDP), while the 'inner periphery' by the definition adopted here has lost its share of both product and population. The 'outer periphery', ie the Homelands, has doubled its share of GNP but this has been accompanied by substantial population growth. The figures for value of product per capita underline the poverty which prevails in the outer periphery; the ratio with the core is still 1:17, despite some improvement (from 1:23) since 1970.

External relations are an important aspect of South Africa's economic geography. Table 4.5 shows the main importers from and exporters to the country. Traditionally the main trading nations were the economically advanced 'western' world, and these are still prominent today despite the emergence of Japan and some other parts of south-east Asia. Figure 4.2 provides a graphic illustration of South Africa's links with the rest of the world through its exports (other than gold). It also emphasises the importance of minerals, especially gold. South Africa has a positive trade balance in Table 4.5 (value of exports exceeded imports by about R13,000 million), but it can easily run into deficit if the price of gold falls, as in the early 1980s.

South Africa's economic relations with neighbouring countries is a further aspect of external interdependence, with important strategic considerations. Malawi, Mozambique and Zimbabwe as well as Botswana, Lesotho and Swaziland all have South Africa as their main trading nation. All have large numbers of their citizens working in South Africa as migrants (see below), and gain substantially

Table 4.4   Geographical distribution of production and population 1970-1986

Area	Production (per cent)		Population (per cent)		Product / capita (Rand)	
	1970	*1986*	*1970*	*1986*	*1970*	*1986*
Metropolitan core	53.6	61.9	33.3	31.0	3050	3601
Inner periphery	44.1	33.1	33.8	26.7	2471	2241
Outer periphery	2.3	5.0	32.9	42.3	131	214

Source: C. J. Meintjes and J. P. Spangenburg (in Van der Kooy, 1988, p. 81). The 'metropolitan core' consists of the PWV area, Durban/Pinetown/Pietermaritzburg, Port Elizabeth/Uitenhage, and the Cape Peninsula; the 'inner periphery' consists of the non-metropolitan areas of the RSA excluding the 'self-governing territories'; the 'outer periphery' consists of the Homelands, ie the TBVC area and the 'self-governing territories'.

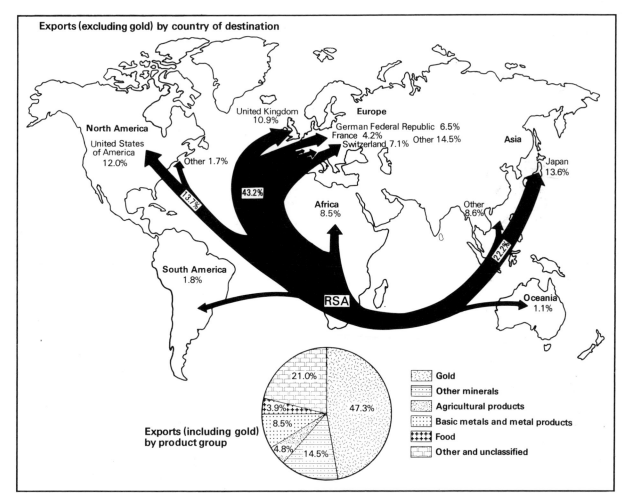

Figure 4.2   Sectoral origin of South Africa's exports and destination of exports (excluding gold), average 1980–1984
Source: **The Debt Standstill and Beyond, Focus on Key Economic Issues,** 38, Merbank (1985).

from the remittances of these workers. Botswana, Lesotho and Swaziland all have well over half their tourists from South Africa. South Africa also supplies crucial materials, including refined oil and electricity, and acts as a conduit for exports especially from Botswana, Lesotho and Zimbabwe. These links help to protect South Africa from what might otherwise be more vigorous antagonism from the so-called 'front-line' states.

Table 4.5   **Top ten importers from and exporters to South Africa 1987**

Importer	Value (R m)	Exporter	Value (R m)
Japan	2,280	West Germany	1,969
Italy	1,791	Japan	1,445
United States	1,420	United Kingdom	1,221
West Germany	1,242	United States	1,002
United Kingdom	1,089	France	362
France	583	Italy	353
Taiwan	451	Taiwan	327
Belgium/Luxembourg	385	Netherlands	224
South Korea	375	Belgium/Luxembourg	219
Hong Kong	325	Switzerland	213
All countries	42,717	All countries	28,736

Source: **Weekly Mail**, 4-10 Aug. 1989, and RSA Trade Statistics.

Foreign investment in South Africa is an important current issue. Capital from overseas is attracted by cheap labour and relatively high profits. Foreign-controlled manufacturing activity involves about 1300 firms employing 400,000 or so workers. Almost 60 per cent of the employment is in firms from the UK and 25 per cent by American firms. In 1987 Britain accounted for about 45 per cent of foreign investment in South Africa, valued at £6000 million, compared with America's £900 million. The largest UK employer in South Africa is Consolidated Gold Fields, with 102,000 workers, followed by ICI with 27,000 and a further twenty or so with at least 2500 employees.

Multinational concerns are sometimes accused of supporting apartheid, from which they benefit in the form of labour which is not only poorly paid but also effectively disenfranchised. However, such firms can also exercise a beneficial influence on employment practices. A report by the British Department of Trade and Industry in 1989 claimed that almost 98 per cent of African workers in British companies were paid above the recommended minimum level of the European Community's Code of Conduct. Others point out that this level is inadequate to ensure decent living standards.

The external orientation of the South African economy is a source of vulnerability as well as strength.

Table 4.6   **Population trends by race group**

	Blacks	Whites	Coloureds	Asians	Total
Increase 1970-88 (1000s)	11,634	1,176	1,076	298	14,184
(per cent)	75.8	31.2	52.5	47.3	65.1
Average annual growth 1987 (per cent)	2.80	0.83	1.92	1.85	2.30
Projected population in 2000 (1000s)	36,037	5,442	3,857	1,134	46,464
Increase 1988-2000 (1000s)	9,063	493	720	206	10,482
Births per 1000 population 1986	40.0	14.9	27.7	22.1	35.0
Deaths per 1000 population 1986	12.0	7.8	8.1	5.5	9.0
Natural increase per 1000 1986	28.0	7.1	19.6	16.6	26.0

Sources: 1988 populations from Table 1.1; growth rate from RSA Department of National Health and Population Development (SAIRR, 1989, p. 149); projections are based on these growth rates and differ slightly from some other sources; birth and death rates from RSA (1989, p. 81) except for the total, from the **United Nations Demographic Yearbook** (1986).

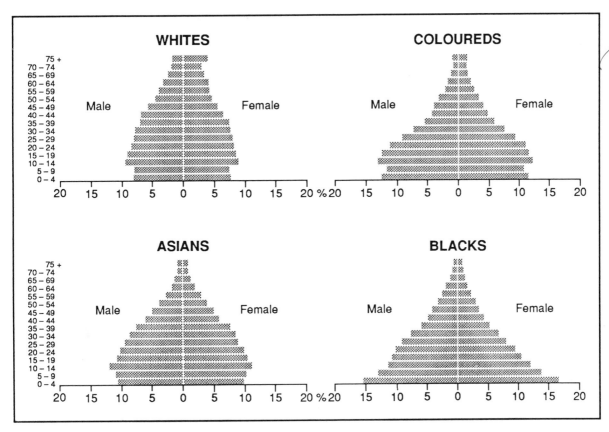

Figure 4.3 Age structure of the population by race group 1985
Source: RSA (1989, p. 85).

Opposition to apartheid from overseas has been expressed in disinvestment or withdrawal of firms from South Africa, and in economic sanctions which include restrictions on trade (considered further in Chapter 6).

Population and employment

The relationship between economic activity and population growth is a crucial ingredient in the employment of labour under apartheid. Taking South Africa as a whole, the supply of labour greatly exceeds the demand generated by the modern sector of the economy, and control of supply is a crucial feature of government policy. Traditionally, this control meant restricting access by Blacks to 'White' areas in general and the core (cities) in particular to numbers consistent with employment opportunities, keeping the rest of the Black population in their peripheral reserves or Homelands. In the notorious words of the 1922 Stallard Commission, 'The native should only be allowed to enter the urban areas, which are essentially the white man's creation, when he is willing to enter and minister to the needs of the white man and should depart therefrom when he ceases so to minister'. There have been some relaxations of strict 'influx control' in the 1980s. but

the gap between the growth of potential Black labour and the capacity of the economy to utilise it remains an acute problem - to Blacks seeking work as well as to the state.

At the heart of what is conventionally viewed as the 'over-supply' of labour is the rate of increase of the Black population. Table 4.6 shows that this was more than twice as high for Blacks as for Whites between 1970 and 1988. The Black population rose by over 11.6 million, the rest of the population by 2.5 million. The high natural increase among Blacks is accounted for by the high birth rate. Population pyramids (Figure 4.3) show 49.7 per cent of Blacks in the age group 0-19 compared with 34.9 per cent of the Whites. More Coloureds are in this age group (48.3 per cent) than Asians (44.5) and the Coloureds have a higher birth rate, but the difference in natural increase is narrowed by the low death rate among Asians.

Population projections for the year 2000 in Table 4.6 show a massive increase in the number of Blacks, especially when compared to that of the Whites. Blacks will then comprise 77.3 per cent of South Africa's total population compared with 74.9 per cent in 1988, while the proportion of Whites will fall from 13.8 per cent to 11.7 in 2000. Other estimates confirm these magnitudes, for example a projection of 47.5 million by 2000 of whom only 6 million will be White, and 74 million with 7 million Whites in 2020 (Bethlehem, 1987, p. 36).

The relationship between Black population and employment prospects in South Africa is thus a matter of great concern. Official figures put the number of Blacks unemployed in the RSA at 823,000 in late 1988, or 13 per cent of those economically active. However, other sources suggest that unemployment is actually much higher - anything up to 5.5 million (**Focus on South Africa**, Dec. 1989, p. 9). There are an additional 350,000 Blacks seeking work each year, compared with an average of roughly 200,000 new jobs being created annually in the latter part of the 1980s. A figure frequently cited is 3.5 million new jobs needed by the year 2000, though one source suggests 6 million which would require job creation at more than double the present rate (Centre for Policy Studies, 1989, pp. 200-1).

If the performance of the economy does not improve, two-thirds of the economically active Black population could be unemployed by the year 2000, compared with perhaps two-fifths today. And to add to the problem, periodic recession and withdrawal of some overseas firms along with sanctions on new investment makes it hard even for the present inadequate level of job creation to be maintained. Thus there is every reason to expect the present substantial shortfall of demand for labour in relation to supply to grow to enormous proportions over the next decade.

This mismatch between labour supply and demand is selective in three important respects. First, it is racially selective, with a disproportionate impact on the rapidly growing Black population, most of whom lack the skills and education to compete for limited employment opportunities. Secondly, it is geographically selective, concentrated in the Homelands and in the Black townships of the 'White' cities. Thirdly, it is qualitatively selective, with the growing sophistication of the economy requiring more skilled jobs while demand for unskilled workers is reduced.

Changes in the kind of labour needed are in fact exacerbating the problem of employment generation. As an economy founded on plentiful cheap (black) labour, South Africa had a much higher proportion of its workforce unskilled in 1980 (58 per cent) and a much lower proportion in professional, technical and managerial occupations (8.8 per cent) than is typical

of advanced economies; the respective proportions in the USA were 5.5 and 32.5 per cent (Bethlehem, 1987, p. 37). Despite Black advances into work previously the province of Whites de facto or (until the end of formal job reservation) de jure, figures for the latter part of the 1980s suggest that there are only about 80,000 Blacks in professional and managerial positions compared with over 1 million Whites, whereas 3.2 million Blacks but only just over 400,000 Whites were workers with varying degrees of skill (**Indicator South Africa**, 4 (1), 1986, p. 107). One recent prediction is of a surplus of over 9 million semi-skilled and unskilled by the end of the century, but a shortage of 200,000 skilled workers (SAIRR, 1989, p. 408); another source even suggests a surplus of skilled workers (C. J. Meintjes and J. P. Spangenburg, in Van der Kooy, 1988, p. 83). Whatever the case may be, those with skills, or able to acquire them, will be at an increasing advantage in the mounting struggle to make a living.

Measures to stimulate economic growth are thus very much on the agenda. These include a programme of 'privatisation' and 'deregulation', designed to improve the performance of the economy by increasing efficiency in the public sector and encouraging private business initiative, much as under the Thatcher government in Britain. However, it is hard to see this having much impact on the central problem, which the influential economist Bethlehem (1987, p. 40) summarises with brutal clarity:

> If economic growth in South Africa does not match population growth, and the experience thus far in the 1980s is discouraging, South Africa will be dragged backwards into the conditions of a Third World country. It is not difficult to imagine a scenario of declining production levels, of food shortages and of deepening misery among the less privileged.

All that needs to be added is that the less privileged, in the core as well as the periphery, are effectively already in the Third World.

Labour supply

The organisation of labour supply may now be examined in more detail. Black labour employed in 'White' South Africa may be divided into three categories: (1) migrant workers, (2) so-called 'frontier commuters' travelling daily from the Homelands, and (3) those who are in effect permanent residents of 'White' South Africa (Figure 4.4). It was for a

47

*Labour storage structures: **Plate 17** (l) Wolhuter municipal hostel for migrant workers in Johannesburg; **Plate 18** (r) hostels in the Diepkloof district of Soweto.*

long time government policy to keep the third category as small as possible and to encourage the maintenance and further development of the other two, consistent with the traditional view of Blacks as merely temporary sojourners whose place is otherwise in their Homeland. While the 1980s have seen some relaxation of this stance (as will be explained below and in Chapter 5), these three categories still capture the essence of the spatial organisation of cheap Black labour.

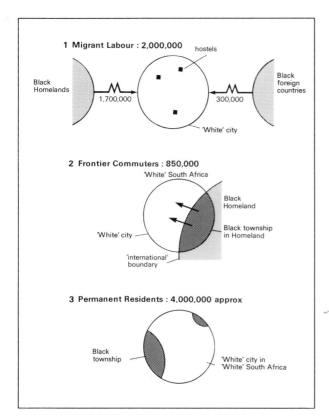

Figure 4.4   Different spatial forms of Black labour in South Africa
Source: approximate figures from tables or text.

The migrant labour system has a long history in South Africa. It was initiated as a means of getting workers into the relatively unpopulated areas of mineral discovery. Its major advantage over other forms of employment is that migrant labour comes cheap, as wages do not necessarily have to cover the support of the family left behind (eg in the Homeland), and costs can be cut further by reducing accommodation and other means of subsistence to a bare minimum consistent with the effective performance of the individual's work. Furthermore, the insecurity of migrant labour tends to constrain organisation and militancy, in the form of trade union activity, with its upward pressure on wages and working conditions.

The traditional pattern, in South Africa, still largely adhered to today, is as follows. The worker lives in a compound, hostel or dormitory, at the mine or other place of employment or provided by a municipality, returning home after completion of the contract (usually of one year's duration) only to leave again shortly for a further contract. The system now involves many workers in manufacturing industry, and this pattern of oscillation between single existence in the 'White' city and brief spells of family life in the Homeland or foreign country is familiar to Blacks all over southern Africa.

In 1986 there were 2.0 million Black migrant workers in 'White' South Africa. Most of them came from the Homelands (Table 4.7): the number has increased by over 700,000 since 1970, and now accounts for about one-third of the total labour force of the Homelands. Over the years covered by the table there has been a steady absolute and relative increase in the numbers from Bophuthatswana and Lebowa and large relative increases from some Homelands which were previously very small suppliers of migrant

Table 4.7　　**Migrant workers from the Homelands 1970-1986 (1000s)**

Homeland of origin	1970	1977	1982	1986
Bophuthatswana	150	179	236	261
Ciskei	52	47	59	60
Transkei	268	263	347	337
Venda	22	26	37	49
Gazankulu	40	39	64	99
KaNgwane	18	29	67	77
KwaNdebele	11	24	52	71
KwaZulu	270	305	294	449
Lebowa	140	140	180	234
QwaQwa	4	43	60	67
Total	975	1095	1395	1704

Sources: 1970 and 1977 from RSA (1983, p. 249), 1982 from SAIRR (1985, p. 258), 1986 from National Manpower Commission (Joyce, 1988, p. 128). Since changes in the law governing Black employment in 1986 removed certain requirements to register, official statistics on migrant labour have not been available.

labour - notably QwaQwa, KwaNdebele and KaNgwane.

As the Homeland supply of migrant workers has increased, so foreign supply has fallen (Table 4.8). The number of Blacks from foreign countries rose to a peak of 836,000 in 1960, and then declined during the period of decolonisation in southern Africa. The mines illustrate how the balance has shifted: in 1964 Blacks from foreign countries accounted for just over 60 per cent of the total mining labour force but figures for 1987 for those employed in gold, platinum, copper and coal mines which were members of the Chamber of Mines show 224,000 of 584,000, or 38

per cent, from foreign sources. While some of the loss can be related to political events in the early 1980s, for example in Mozambique, the most dramatic reduction was from Malawi following an air crash in 1974 in which a large number of Malawi migrant workers were killed and which led to the suspension of recruitment.

The continuing reliance of the mines on migrant labour is illustrated by the fact that in 1987 there were 529,000 such workers in gold and coal mines which were members of the Chamber of Mines, compared with the total of 584,000 which included those in platinum or copper (SAIRR, 1988, pp. 335-6; 1989,

Table 4.8　　**Migrant workers from foreign countries 1973-1986 (1000s)**

Country of origin	1973	1977	1983	1986
Bostswana	46	43	30	28
Lesotho	149	161	146	138
Malawi	140	13	30	31
Mozambique	127	111	61	73
Swaziland	10	21	17	22
Zimbabwe	3	33	8	7
Total (including others)	486	392	359	303

Source: 1973 and 1977 from A. Lemon (in Smith, 1982, p. 69), 1983 from RSA (1985, p. 220), 1986 from SAIRR (1988, pp. 312-3). Note that the 1983 total is inflated by the inclusion of Namibia among 'others'; the total without 'others' is 292,000 in 1983 compared with 475,000 in 1973, 382,000 in 1977 and 299,000 in 1986.

*The 'White' city: **Plate 19** (l) central Johannesburg, from which blacks are supposedly excluded except as workers; **Plate 20** (r) central Durban, with 'Kombi' taxis waiting to take black commuters home to the townships and shack areas on the fringe of the city.*

pp. 420-1). Despite improvements in living conditions for migrant workers, some mining companies still respond to pressure for more family housing by maintaining that it is five times more expensive than keeping the individual worker in a hostel. The migrant labour system continues to be criticised on humanitarian grounds, and is increasingly at odds with the needs of mining as well as manufacturing for a more skilled, reliable and settled labour force. The granting of much-coveted blasting certificates to the first Black miners at the end of 1988 was an important symbol of entry to skilled work which had previously been reserved for Whites (and the final act in abolishing job reservation).

The second category of Black labour is that of the frontier commuter, defined as Blacks who reside in the Homelands but travel daily to work in the cities, industrial districts or rural areas of 'White' South Africa. In apartheid thinking, they thus commute across what is now (in the case of 'independent republics') or what may eventually be (in the case of the remaining 'self-governing territories') an international boundary.

The beginning of frontier commuting as an explicit element in apartheid planning strategy was associated with an important change in policy over Black townships. In 1967 local authorities were required to obtain central government approval before initiating any new Black housing schemes, the intention being to prevent further townships being set up in 'White' South Africa if they could be established in a conveniently situated part of a Homeland. From 1968 (until subsequent relaxations, considered in the next chapter), Blacks were allowed only to rent houses in townships in 'White' South Africa, whereas in the Homeland they could buy, thus encouraging Blacks to move to Homeland townships.

The Homeland locations helped to externalise costs of social welfare support, which could be conveyed as the responsibility of the government of the existing or future Black independent state, thus relieving the RSA and its employers of some of the cost of labour in its full sense. This strategy was also consistent with the transfer of Black political aspirations from where people actually worked to their places of residence over the 'border'. In fact, frontier commuting preserved some of the advantages of migrant labour, while enabling workers to live a fairly normal settled community and family life not far from their place of employment.

Table 4.9 shows the enormous increase in frontier commuting during the 1970s and first half of the 1980s (since when comparable data have not been available). Assuming trends in the second half of the 1980s similar to those in the first half, there could be something approaching a million Blacks involved today. The pre-eminence of Bophuthatswana and KwaZulu reflects the proximity of parts of these Homelands to cities in 'White' South Africa. The largest commuter flows are from Bophuthatswana into Pretoria and from KwaZulu into Durban.

The third category of Black worker lives, in effect, permanently in 'White' South Africa. In traditional apartheid terminology, they are 'permanently absent' from their Homeland. Official figures for 1980 placed their number at almost exactly 3 million, but the subsequent increase plus an allowance for under-enumeration suggests something more like 4 million Black workers living permanently in 'White' South Africa. These are the inhabitants of the townships which are not in the Homelands, and of the rural areas of 'White' South Africa. They are the major inconsistency in the old concept of a White Republic, for their presence is necessary to the functioning of

Table 4.9 **Frontier commuters from the Homelands into 'White' South Africa 1970-1985 (1000s)**

Homeland of origin	1970	1976	1979	1982	1985
Bophuthatswana	84	136	155	173	
Ciskei	40	34	37	38	
Transkei	3	7	9	8	
Venda	3	4	6	6	
Gazankulu	3	6	8	8	9
KaNgwane	3	23	33	44	47
KwaNdebele	0	0	4	12	20
KwaZulu	127	279	352	395	432
Lebowa	26	44	58	76	76
QwaQwa	1	2	3	12	2
Total	291	536	664	773	

Sources: 1970 from Bureau of Economic Development and Research, courtesy A. Lemon; 1976 and 1979 from Zingel (1985, p. 4); 1982 from SAIRR (1985, pp. 258-9); 1985 from RSA (1989, p. 175). Note that different sources provide somewhat different figures for some years; those above reflect what appear to be the most authoritative. No data are available for the TBVC for 1985, but if commuting had increased by the same proportion as for the six other Homelands since 1982 the total for 1985 would have been about 850,000. Since changes in the law governing Black employment in 1986, the recording of frontier commuters has become more difficult and official figures are no longer published. The Development Bank of Southern Africa gives the 1985 total as 768,000 (**Indicator South Africa**, 6 (2), p. 62). Joyce (1988, p. 128) provides figures for 1986 totalling 507,000, but it is hard to reconcile this with the ealier data which themselves may underestimate the actual numbers of Blacks crossing Homeland boundaries to work.

the economy. While they may still be portrayed in more conservative White politics as belonging to some Homeland, links may be tenuous at best: most Blacks living in 'White' areas have been born there, and have neither children nor parents living in a Homeland. The South African government has now recognised this, and that the Republic of South Africa will continue to have a large, permanent Black population.

It is in the major economic heartland of the PWV that the inconsistency between traditional apartheid thinking and actual practice is revealed most clearly. While Pretoria has its own townships of Atteridgeville and Mamelodi inherited from the pre-1967 era (see Figure 5.1 in Chapter 5), it is close enough to part of Bophuthatswana to take advantage of frontier commuting. Large townships have been built within the 'independent republic' of Bophuthatswana, as displaced dormitories for Black workers employed in Pretoria. However, the Witwatersrand is too far from Bophuthatswana or any other Homeland to take advantage of large-scale frontier commuting. The Black labour not provided by migrants must therefore have places of residence in 'White' territory: hence the existence of massive townships such as Soweto, here and around Vereeniging to the south.

This discussion should have helped further to clarify the role of the Homelands in the grand design of classical apartheid. Applying the estimated Black activity rate of one in three to the 1988 Homeland population of 13.8 million gives about 4.2 million economically active. Tables 4.7 and 4.9 suggest that over 2.5 million are migrant workers or frontier commuters, so a majority of the working population of the ten Homelands is employed in 'White' South Africa. The degree of economic dependence on those who work outside is illustrated by 1985 figures for the six excluding the TBVC area, which show Gross National Product exceeding Gross Domestic Produce from 2.3 times for Gazankulu and 3.0 for Lebowa up to 4.5 for KaNgwane and 7.9 times for KwaNdebele. The four 'independent republics' also rely heavily on income from their residents working in the RSA. The relative importance of frontier commuters and migrants varies considerably, from Bophuthatswana's high commuter income, through KwaZulu where both are very important, to the Transkei's extreme reliance on migrants. Most domestically generated Homeland income comes from agriculture and without the external sources poverty would be universal and extreme. The migrant and commuter incomes themselves are deceptive when attributed to the Homelands, for a substantial proportion are spent where they are earned, in the cities of the RSA.

The past decade has seen some restructuring of the spatial organisation of Black labour supply associated with the Homeland strategy. This has been designed to reduce market rigidities in the interests of promoting faster economic growth by the more efficient deployment of labour. The process was initiated by two Commissions which reported at the end of the 1970s. The Wiehahn Commission investigated labour law, and recommended the recognition and registration of African trade unions, thus paving the way for more open and effective labour organisation in the 1980s - albeit with firm state control. The Riekert Commission considered labour recruitment, influx control, and how industry could improve access to the workers it needed. In the words of the Riekert Report (1979, cited in Unterhalter, 1987, p. 24): 'It is a prerequisite for sound economic growth in South Africa for employers to be able to satisfy their full labour requirements and for adequate job opportunities to be created for the country's fast-growing labour force. ... the necessary machinery must be used to ensure that the supply and demand for Black labour are brought into equilibrium'. What was proposed was clearly not so much a freeing of the labour market as a new form of control.

Briefly, the outcome was measures to give greater residential security in the 'White' cities to certain kinds of Black workers (those with skills, and most in demand), along with more freedom to move about in search of jobs. This involved important changes in policy on influx control and Black urbanisation, which will be considered in the next chapter. However, other workers, mainly the unskilled, would remain migrants with no prospect of establishing residence rights in the cities. A distinction was made between the 'insiders', to whom the prospect of a permanent place and enhanced opportunities within the RSA has been given, and the 'outsiders' kept at bay by regulatory devices and Homeland boundaries.

Francis Wilson has likened the spatial political economy of labour supply in southern Africa to an onion, illustrated in Figure 4.5, with a central core surrounded by a number of rings. The core represents the mines and factories, towns and cities of South Africa, surrounded by the White farming areas. The first ring around this core represents the non-independent Homelands, the second the 'independent' Homelands, the next the former High Commission Territories of Botswana, Lesotho and Swaziland, and finally the states beyond. Each of the layers has

a successively greater degree of formal political independence from South Africa.

Wilson relates these political entities to labour links. For much of this century the political boundaries separating the different layers from the core were not particularly significant: South Africa drew its labour, in the form of migrants, from large parts of southern Africa with little trouble. As political change took place to the north, with countries in the outer layers peeling off as far as South Africa's de facto control was concerned, dependence on foreign migrants was reduced (as was shown above). The emphasis shifted to reinforcing boundaries closer to the core. The problems of population growth, unemployment and poverty in the Homelands are externalised by their 'independence' and a restructuring of influx control. The cheap labour produced in the Homelands is admitted to the core as demand requires, through the medium of frontier commuting as well as migrant workers. Once in the core, the mobility of workers between sectors and localities is facilitated by reforms of legislation governing Black labour affairs, initiated by the Wiehahn and Riekert Commissions. Those Blacks who are now recognised as permanent residents of the core of South Africa have become a kind of lower labour aristocracy, with a level of living conspicuously superior to that of Blacks in the Homeland labour reserves but inferior to that of the White working class (higher labour aristocracy) whose continuing support for the government is still to some extent based on economic advantage associated with racial privilege.

Wilson's analogy helps, again, to see the role of the Homelands in a broader context. Both the partial externalisation of labour costs and effective influx control are facilitated by 'independence', which is in this sense not the fiction that some opponents of apartheid claim. It serves a specific purpose more effectively than if these territories were politically integral to the Republic of South Africa. The continuation of this role depends on Homeland leadership compliant with South Africa's purpose, at least in the 'independent republics', on which there is growing uncertainty (especially in Transkei). It also depends on how much of the traditional and restructured geo-political economy of labour supply can survive the further incorporation of the Black population into South Africa's political institutions.

The informal sector

For those people unable to get jobs in the factories,

52

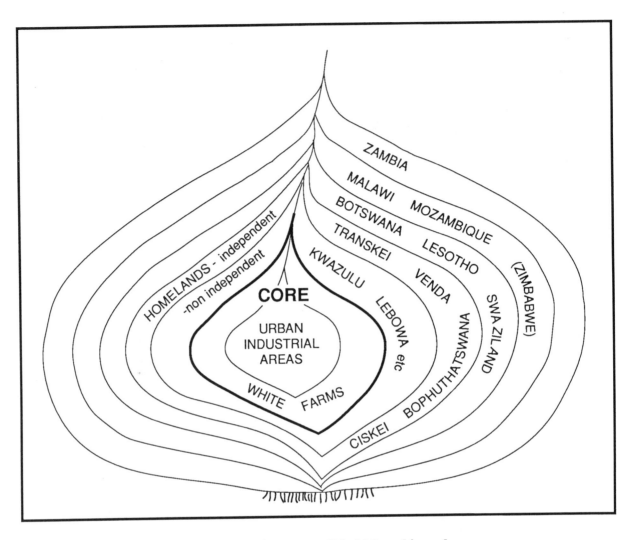

Figure 4.5   The onion analogy of South Africa's geo-political labour hierarchy
Source: redrawn from Zingel (1985, p. 2), after F. Wilson in **South Africa Outlook**, March 1980.

farms, mines and offices of the formal economy, the 'informal sector' may provide an alternative. The informal sector, in its strict sense, refers to unlicensed and unrecorded activities, and has been part of the economic structure of South Africa for a long time. However, its scale and scope has increased considerably in recent years, and it is today very much a feature of the urban economy. The reasons for the growth of the informal sector include the decline in agricultural employment, the large-scale rural to urban shift of the Black population, a fall in real earnings which has forced families to seek alternative sources of income, and the unemployment which so greatly afflicts Black people.

The kind of activities found in the informal sector in South Africa include retailing (eg street peddling, hawking, food stalls, small shops, soft drink distribution and sale, flower selling, and informal drinking places or 'shebeens'), services (eg shoe repairing, taxi transport, domestic work and child minding), manufacturing (eg building trades, knitting, brewing liquor), and also gambling, drug vending and prostitution. The form of organisation ranges from street-side selling of vegetables and so on from a single basket or box, to cooperatives and chains in some branches which rival parts of the formal sector in their scale and sophistication. In fact, the distinction between the informal and formal sector is not always easy to establish. Historically, the authorities discouraged and strictly controlled the informal sector (Rogerson and Beavon, 1980), but this kind of economic activity is now increasingly recognised as providing a solution to some of the country's employment problem.

Recent estimates of the scale of the informal sector vary considerably (eg SAIRR, 1989, pp. 357-9). In 1988 the Small Business Development Corporation suggested a figure of 625,000 unrecorded, unlicensed, non-taxable informal sector businesses. They put the number of people engaged full or part-time at up to

The informal sector of the economy: **Plate 21** *(l) street-side sales near a formal shopping centre in Takoza on the Witwatersrand;* **Plate 22** *(r) small shop in the shack area of Inanda on the border of the city of Durban and KwaZulu.*

4 million, and say that the informal sector could be accounting for as many as 150,000 of the 350,000 people entering the job market every year. Confirmation of the overall magnitude is provided by Ian Hetherington of Job Creation South Africa, who claims that the formal and informal sectors both employ about 4 million Blacks. A somewhat lower figure, of about 2 million, was arrived at by the Development Bank of Southern Africa in 1985; they identified the sub-sectors as trading and hawking (55 per cent), production and construction (23 per cent), services (16 per cent) and 'illegitimate activities' (6 per cent), with average earnings of R350 per month.

The government claims that the informal sector produces goods and services equivalent to 3-4 per cent of the formal sector's output, but there are claims that it could be ten times these figures. The consensus ranges between 10 and 20 per cent of Gross Domestic Product (**Sunday Times, Business Times**, 21 May 1989). The Reserve Bank believes that the informal sector could account for a third of Black incomes. While it is the involvement of Blacks/Africans that has attracted most attention, there are also Coloureds and Indians involved, and many Whites run small businesses from their homes; what is sometimes known in Britain as the 'black economy' is by no means racially exclusive in South Africa.

The growth of the informal sector has been associated with the rise of informal or spontaneous settlement (see next chapter). For example, when Crossroads was consolidating on the edge of Cape Town towards the end of the 1970s, a survey identified 116 businesses there, most of them in retailing with cafes and food shops predominating. Manufacturing activities included the production of clothing, knitwear and tin trunks. Only half the incomes generated reached R200 a month and a quarter less than R100, figures

roughly representative of what might then be earned in the mines and domestic service respectively.

An important feature of the growth of retailing in Black areas is the so-called 'spaza' (or camouflaged) shop. These operate, more or less discreetly, from people's homes or garages; many were set up as a result of boycotts of White business. There are an estimated 20,000 spazas on the Witwatersrand alone, and it has been suggested that, taken together, their combined purchasing power would make them a contender to join the three big supermarket chains in South Africa. Something of the character of these businesses is captured in the following description of the huge Black residential complex of Khayelitsha in the western Cape (Vuyo Bavumo in the **Weekend Argus**, 22 July 1989):

> A network of thriving back-yard shops has risen to challenge the poverty in the sprawling squatter camp. The shops, known as 'spazas', are informal businesses which operate from iron and wood shacks. They provide work and area service for the community. Some generate a turnover of between R35,000 and R50,000 a month. Most sell, among other things, blankets, primus stoves, meat and other basic foods. Some act as a post office. And the hours are long - most stay open from 7am to 8pm. Because electricity is not supplied to the area, many owners use diesel generators to run their refrigerators. Unlike conventional stores, they do not pay rents for their businesses. Like other residents, the owners paid a R25 fee for erecting a shack. Because of their accessibility, the 30 shops in the area have proved to be popular. And their prices compare favourable with the supermarkets that are much further away. Some of the stores have well-stocked shelves

with coloured boards advertising their latest 'specials' on their doors.

Informal production and trading is now widespread throughout Black settlements of whatever kind. For example, surveys suggest that anything from one-tenth to one-third of households in Soweto participate in the informal sector. While many traders operate within Soweto, others travel into Johannesburg to sell their wares at the transport termini and other places through which large numbers of Black commuters pass. Similarly in Durban, where informal traders are joining the traditional early morning market near the city centre, described as follows by Ismail Suder (**Daily News**, 10 Aug. 1989):

> More than 350 informal squatters take their place outside the market each morning at 5.30am to sell their wares which range from boiled sheep hearts to second hand shoes. ... two women sit on an upturned milk crate, selling fried chicken pieces - prepared on the pavement - for R1.30 a piece. A customer sits nearby on his haunches eating some of the wares, throwing the bones at his feet. In the parking lot, fruit and vegetables are stacked high on pallets.

These newcomers are resented by the formal market traders, on grounds including hygiene, just as White businesses have traditionally been hostile to Black competition in trade - formal or informal.

One important business which straddles the formal/informal divide is that of 'Kombi' or minibus taxis. This has grown enormously in recent years, with the number of vehicles involved estimated at between 70,000 and 125,000 (SAIRR, 1989, p. 366). The major stimulus has come from increased Black commuting, including the frontier version. Kombis offer residents of often dispersed Black settlements a more flexible means of moving to and from work than buses and trains, and they also provide protection from the criminals who operate on public transport. Many Kombis trade formally, with registration which requires checks for mechanical reliability; many do not. They have enabled Blacks to set up businesses on their own account, though Whites are also involved in funding the purchase of vehicles and in the organisation of some taxi firms.

Another activity which is hard to categorise with respect to degree of formality is domestic service. There may be a million domestic workers in South Africa (SAIRR, 1989, p. 429), employed to clean the house, cook, look after children and tend the garden. Figures for 1985-87 from the Central Statistical Service show that 78.3 per cent were African females, 11.1 per cent Coloured females, 9.6 per cent African males, and 0.1 per cent White males (**Weekly Mail**, 11-17 Aug. 1989). Over two-thirds of White South African households employ domestic workers, and in some areas (eg Pretoria, Durban, Pietermaritzburg and East London), about a quarter employ two or more. While some White families take on responsibilities for their domestics and their families well beyond the payment of wages, domestic work usually involves long hours, long journeys from townships to White suburbs, insecure employment, and low pay. No other aspect of labour in South Africa more vividly illustrated the unequal economic relations between the races.

5 URBAN AND REGIONAL DEVELOPMENT

'These restless broken streets where definitions fail ...' (Nadine Gordimer, 1979)

That apartheid produces some distinctive urban and regional forms will be apparent from earlier chapters. This is not surprising in a society in which the (Black) majority of the population have traditionally been regarded as rural outsiders, given access to urban areas only to minister to the Whites, and in which urban and regional planning has had racial separation as a major objective. And even as circumstances change, with the government's recognition of a large and permanent Black presence in the cities, the emerging spatial forms have peculiarities which express a continuing failure to see full political and social integration as the inevitable accompaniment of a modern racially integrated economy. This chapter brings some of the themes from earlier discussions together with recent trends in urban and regional development policy and practice, to fill out and round off the interpretations initiated in Chapter 3.

Urbanisation

From the earliest stages, the White population of what was to become South Africa concentrated in towns. The ports grew as necessary links with Europe, and the subsequent exploitation of minerals involved a highly localised form of settlement. There was also security from the 'natives' to consider, with the prefix of Fort to some place names indicating their defensive origin. The emergence of farming enclaves in the coastal areas, along with the Boer 'treks' into the interior, created a more dispersed population distribution. But the image of the town surrounded by alien territory and tribes, and for Afrikaners their 'laager' formed by a circle of wagons protecting its people, is a powerful evocation of South Africa's turbulent and often violent settlement of a land which had from the outset been contested.

By the beginning of the present century just over half the White population of South Africa was officially classified as urban. There were also 350,000 Africans in urban areas, although this accounted for barely 10 per cent of their total population. As numbers of Africans grew, so did the shanty-town slums on the edges of the towns and cities. Slum clearance and township construction brought the system under some degree of order, while the introduction of formal measures of influx control kept inward migration to manageable numbers. More recently, however, there have been important new developments, including the urbanisation of the Homelands associated largely with frontier commuting, and certain features of Third-World urbanisation have reasserted themselves in a way that defies the authorities' power to control the formation of South Africa's cities and metropolitan regions. Urbanisation in South Africa is thus both a product of apartheid and a challenge to its future.

The polarised space-economy of South Africa is reflected in a marked concentration of urban population. The seven largest urban areas as officially enumerated, each with a population of over half a million, together account for a little more than 7 million people, roughly a quarter of the total in the RSA (Table 1.2 in Chapter 1), and this is likely to be a substantial underestimate of the true figures. However, it is more realistic to consider the Pretoria/Witwatersrand/Vereeniging area as a singe loose conurbation, dominating the population distribution. With Durban/Pinetown, the Cape Peninsula and Port Elizabeth/Uitenhage, the PWV accounts for 70 per cent of the Republic's urban population, along with 76 per cent of mining and industrial employment and 80 per cent of industrial output.

Table 5.1 shows the increasing urbanisation of the population of each race group. The proportion of Whites and Asians/Indians in urban areas by 1985 resembled that of the population of the advanced industrial nations of the world. The Coloured figure is also high; the fact that this group has not urbanised at the same pace as the Asians is explained by the more rapid displacement of the latter from agriculture. The most significant feature, however, is the increase in the proportion of the Black/African population in urban areas. This started from a very low base, and remains low when compared with the other groups despite the accelerating pace of Black urbanisation in recent years. The present proportion may be nearer 60 per cent than the official figure of barely 40 per cent, if under-enumeration is taken into account.

For most of the Black population of the cities, home is in one of the townships: unknown territory to most Whites (Beavon, 1982). The largest is Soweto, which has come to symbolise the environment imposed on urban Blacks, and their resistance to it. The actual population of Soweto exceeds 1.5 million,

Table 5.1   **Urbanisation by race group (per cent of total population) 1904-1985**

Year	Whites	Coloureds	Asians	Blacks
1904	53.6	49.2	36.4	10.4
1911	53.0	50.4	52.8	13.0
1921	59.7	52.4	60.4	14.0
1936	68.2	58.0	69.5	19.0
1946	75.6	62.5	72.8	24.3
1951	79.1	66.2	77.6	27.9
1960	83.6	68.3	83.2	31.8
1970	86.7	74.3	86.2	33.0
1980	87.9	75.2	89.8	37.9
1985	89.6	77.8	93.4	39.6

Source: RSA (1989, p. 88).

its official population being swelled by hundreds of thousands of illegal residents. About 250,000 people travel into Johannesburg daily, by rail, bus or 'Kombi' taxi. Major programmes to improve living conditions have been initiated since riots in 1976, including bringing electricity into 90 per cent of houses. However, services remain poorly developed and public facilities very limited indeed for a city of this size. For example, there are only 13 soccer fields, 10 clinics and 4 libraries (Mashabela, 1988, p. 150), refuse clearance is insufficient to prevent it piling up on the roadside, and two-thirds of the road surfaces are still gravel, with only 10 per cent with stormwater drainage (SAIRR **Social and Economic Update**, 7, 1989, p. 41). There are high rates of crime against persons and property to add to the pervading poverty, social deprivation and environmental degradation.

Rapid expansion of the Black population in South Africa's major metropolitan areas is predicted by the end of the century, with annual growth rates of 3-5 per cent or more (Table 5.2). The PWV and greater Durban will have the largest concentrations, with 12 million between them. A total Black urban population of 26.2 million by the year 2000 has been predicted, 60 per cent of the growth arising from natural increase (SAIRR, 1989, pp. 156-7). Thus massive growth is built into the present urban population, without taking into account further migration from the countryside.

Table 5.2   **African population of major metropolitan areas 1987-2000**

Area	1987 (1000s)	2000 (1000s)	Annual growth (per cent)
Bloemfontein	200	330	4.0
Cape Town	422	858	5.6
Durban	2,558	4,103	3.7
East London	308	507	3.9
Kimberley	89	145	3.8
Orange Free State Goldfields	115	219	5.1
Pietermaritzburg	300	481	3.7
Port Elizabeth/Uitenhage	512	978	4.4
Pretoria/Witwatersrand/Vereeniging	4,852	7,978	3.9
Total	9,076	15,600	4.1

Source: SAIRR (1989, p. 157), following Urban Foundation (figures rounded).

*Two sides of Soweto: **Plate 23** (l) the early township landscape of uniform housing; **Plate 24** (r) upper-income enclave in Diepkloof for members of the emerging Black elite.*

A major trend which became apparent during the 1970s was urbanisation of parts of the Homelands. This began as central government policy in the 1960s, after the influx control measures introduced in the 1950s had failed to reduce African population pressures in what was looked on as 'White' South Africa, in the face of the decline of subsistence agriculture in the Homelands and the expansion of manufacturing in the cities. Homeland urbanisation was closely associated with attempts to disperse industry to locations close to their borders (see section on regional planning below).

At first the new townships 'proclaimed' (ie officially established) in the Homelands were seen as ways of side-tracking potential rural migrants to the 'White' towns and cities, and of resettling Blacks from 'White' rural as well as urban areas. This was followed by the effective freezing of the construction of family housing for Blacks in 'White' areas from the beginning of 1968, and the development of townships in the Homelands as dormitories for frontier commuters. Associated with this strategy was the 'deproclamation' of some townships outside the Homelands, to prevent further settlement there and to facilitate the 'repatriation' of their residents to the new townships across the border. However, some of the apparent increase in Homeland urban population was simply a result of boundary changes, such as the incorporation of Umlazi and KwaMashu into KwaZulu. That these trends in Black urban settlement were closely associated with a spatial restructuring of labour supply will be apparent from the discussion in the previous chapter.

Between 1970 and 1981 the number of housing units in proclaimed townships in the Homelands increased from about 80,000 to almost 200,000, and the population within them from 525,000 to almost 1,500,000 (RSA, 1983, p. 247; SAIRR, 1983, pp. 439-40). These figures suggest that around 15 per cent of the Homeland population was living in these urban areas by the early 1980s. However, the subsequent decade has seen important changes in the nature of 'urbanisation' in the Homelands, with the meaning of 'urban' itself becoming blurred. Rural areas near the townships or borders with 'White' South Africa have been filling up with what are sometimes referred to as 'closer settlements', where people live at urban densities in what might otherwise be considered a rural environment but without access to arable or grazing land. And formal township construction has given way to informal settlement as the predominant means of Homeland urbanisation (see next section).

Table 5.3 provides two alternative estimates of the scale and nature of urbanisation in the Homelands, with predictions to the year 2000. The differences between them, in definitions as well as numbers, indicate that neither categories nor counting are straightforward. The most striking feature is that the peri-urban or urban fringe areas are shown as matching the proclaimed townships in population growth. Taking both as urban, the proportion of total Homeland population has increased from 22 per cent in 1970 to 28 per cent in 1980, and 45 per cent is projected by the year 2000 when only about 55 per cent will be strictly rural.

South Africa's urban settlement pattern must now be viewed at a regional scale rather than as a matter of individual city morphology. Davies (1981) has drawn attention to the creation of the 'apartheid city' as more systematically divided up racially than the 'segregation city' which preceded it (see Lemon, 1987, pp. 220-1 for diagrammatic representations, and Simon, 1989, pp. 192-3 for a suggestion of an

Table 5.3   **Homeland urbanisation: population estimates and projections to the year 2000 (1000s)**

by J. Graaf	Urban	Peri-urban	Semi-rural	Rural	Total
1980	1,953	1,853	1,082	6,912	11,801
2000	4,872	4,131	1,694	9,496	20,193

by C. Simkins	Urban	Urban fringe		Rural	Total
1970	775	866		5,841	7,483
1980	1,490	1,454		7,775	10,719
1990*	1,920	1,860		8.950	12,730
	2,710	2,630		10,110	15,450
2000*	3,940	3,830		9,340	17,110
	4,030	3,920		10,660	18,610

Sources: O. Crankshaw and T. Hart, Human Sciences Research Council (original figures rounded). Graaf and Simkins both define 'urban' as proclaimed townships; Graaf defines 'peri-urban' as significantly dependent on commuting, 'semi-rural' as concentrations of more than 5000 people, and 'rural' as the remainder; Simkins defines 'urban fringe' as Homeland districts adjacent to metropolitan areas and 'rural' as landed and landless rural communities; * indicates that there are two estimates based on different growth rate assumptions.

updated version). In Figure 5.1 the Pretoria case of the apartheid city is shown, with its Group Areas and White space differentiated by economic status, as Davies suggested. The Bophuthatswana Homeland (or 'independent republic') is also shown, with the large townships of Garankuwa, Mabopane and Temba (with its industrial area of Babelegi) just within its borders. The township of Soshanguve lies just inside the RSA; it is served by the same new railway as Mabopane and about 100,000 commuters travel the 25 km into Pretoria non-stop each day. Informal settlements, notably at Winterveld, form part of the displaced urban agglomeration which, in 'normal' circumstances, would have grown up by contiguous extensions of the city of Pretoria. Their total population today is estimated at approaching a million, not much short of half the population of Bophuthatswana.

Informal settlement

One of the most important features of contemporary urbanisation in South Africa is informal or 'shack' settlement. Sometimes referred to as spontaneous, or as squatter settlement in recognition of its often illegal occupation of land, informal settlement is widespread around cities throughout the Third World. There were shanty towns on the edges of some South African cities at the beginning of the apartheid era, but they were eliminated, for the most part, as their residents were rehoused in the new townships. But

the restrictions on township construction initiated in the late 1960s, coupled with natural population increase on the part of Blacks already in the cities as well as continuing migration from the countryside, led to a resurgence of spontaneous settlement in the 1970s. By the end of the decade almost every city had its satellite informal settlement, and they were also growing in some of the Homelands as resettlement gathered pace (Unterhalter, 1987, pp. 85-92).

The number of people involved is of course hard to state accurately. One recent estimate suggests at least 7 million people living in 'squatter' settlements, backyards and garages (**Focus on South Africa**, Nov. 1989, citing S. F. Coetzee of the Development Bank), compared with the figure of about 4 million commonly adopted in the mid-1980s. Most of the people involved are Blacks/Africans, but there are also substantial numbers of Coloureds and some Indians in informal settlements. The proportion of South Africa's Blacks living in spontaneous settlements may now be around 25 per cent.

Table 5.4 offers estimates for some particular areas. The very low figures provided by the relevant government department, except for the PWV area, indicates official reluctance to accept the scale of this conspicuous failure to provide housing within the formal sector, along with differences in definition. However, a figure of 1.3 million African squatters in South Africa has been conceded (SAIRR, 1988, p.

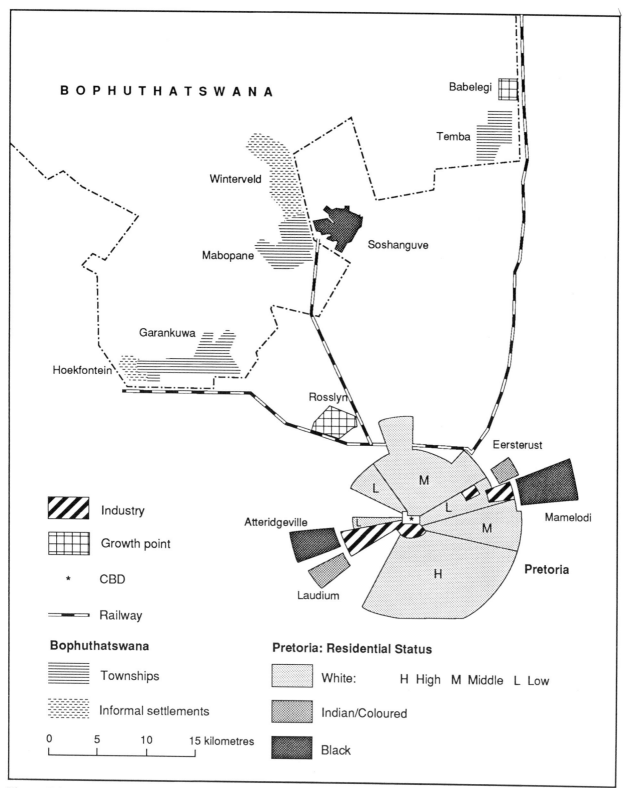

Figure 5.1 **Urbanisation under apartheid: Pretoria and part of Bophuthatswana**
Source: J. J. Olivier and P. S. Hattingh (in Smit, 1985, p. 14).

197). Other areas not listed in the table include Botshabelo to the east of Bloemfontein (mentioned in Chapter 2), where the population is estimated to be up to 500,000.

The essence of spontaneous settlement is usually that people occupy land without authorisation, and construct their own homes out of whatever material may be readily available. In South Africa this takes the form of in-filling in existing formal residential areas by building shacks in back yards or on any vacant site, as well as entirely informal settlements. And it can also involve Black occupation of small dwellings built for servants in the gardens of White

Informal or shack settlement: **Plate 25** *(l) Inanda on the edge of Durban;* **Plate 26** *(r) Khayelitsha in the Western Cape.*

areas. The quality of accommodation varies considerably, with building material and opportunities for upgrading. Informal settlements are usually far more organised, by their own inhabitants, than might be suggested by their superficially chaotic appearance.

Such settlements arise, quite simply, from the shortage of formal housing in the right place and at a price or rental that people can afford - itself a reflection of a highly unequal society. Informal settlements enable Blacks who could not otherwise live in or near the cities to gain entry, in circumstances where their presence, if illegal, is hard to detect. They also provide the opportunity for family life for men working in 'White' South Africa unable to obtain formal housing. They can, in fact, offer Blacks greater comfort and personal freedom than living in the highly congested townships or compounds, where the authorities exercise a high degree of control. These settlements are also to the advantage of White employers (industrial and domestic), as they enable part of the Homeland labour reserve to be transferred to a location convenient to the metropolitan labour

market, yet lacking the security, permanence and expense of a formal township.

Something of the nature of informal settlement is captured as follows by Bernstein (1989, p. 19):

A typical community is situated 35 kilometres south of Johannesburg, next to a paved road and bus route. The land is privately owned in a peri-urban area surrounded by smallholdings and a new housing development extending from a nearby residential area. There are 450 shacks in the community, all of which are owner-built and occupied. Most shacks are constructed of corrugated iron, although there are numerous mud and wattle houses and a few breeze-block structures. The cost of construction ranges from R300 to R1000.

The settlement, established totally informally, is now home for a group of people who for the most part have been

Table 5.4   Alternative estimates of population of informal settlements 1987

Area	Department of Constitutional Development and Planning	Urban Foundation
Durban/Pinetown	3,353	1,700,000
Eastern Cape	11,560	200,000
KwaNdebele		350,000
Pretoria/Witwatersrand/Vereeniging	914,101	1,600,000-2,400,000
Western Cape	6,784	400,000
Winterveld (Bophuthatswana)		600,000
Total		4,850,000-5,650,000

Source: SAIRR (1989, p. 162).

forced to lead a nomadic existence moving between farms, townships and shack areas in the southern PWV region. The residential histories of the inhabitants reflect the broader national trends of black exclusion from white agricultural areas, the stagnation of urban development for black South Africans, and removals occasioned by the racial zoning and rezoning of residential and peri-urban land.

Against this background, an informal 'town' has been created through individual and community tenacity and resourcefulness in the face of pervasive insecurity. Close examination reveals that the settlement has many of the characteristics of a planned and managed urban place.

Three local cases may be used further to illustrate spontaneous settlement in South Africa. The first is the Western Cape, where there are large areas of spontaneous settlement in the Cape Town metropolitan area and beyond. Spontaneous settlements have been erected mainly by Blacks, but there are also some Coloureds involved. The former are unable or unwilling to live in the townships or hostels. The latter have resorted to spontaneous settlement because of the shortage and overcrowding of formal housing for Coloureds. Estimates of the population in spontaneous settlements at the end of the 1970s suggest a figure of 180,000; today it could be half a million.

The settlement known as Crossroads has become a *cause célèbre*, drawing international attention to spontaneous settlement in South Africa and to the government's initially unsympathetic and brutal response. Crossroads is on the eastern edge of Cape Town (Figure 1.2 in Chapter 1) and adjoins the Black township of Nyanga. By the end of the 1970s it had a population of 20-25,000 living in over 3000 self-constructed structures. Far from being a shiftless mass of unemployed and illegal immigrants, crime-prone and a threat to social order, which is how the government sought to portray the inhabitants of spontaneous settlements, those in Crossroads were found to be for the most part a stable element in the workforce, necessary to the city economy.

In 1982 the population of Crossroads was estimated to have risen to 60,000, having survived by virtue of the publicity which its possible destruction attracted and through the tenacity of its residents. The Minister of Cooperation and Development (ie Black affairs) had agreed to build a new township for the inhabitants in the vicinity of Crossroads, but in 1983 this was overtaken by a proposal both more ambitious and more significant to Black urbanisation policy. The plan was to create a new city of 200-300,000 for all Blacks legally resident in the Cape Town metropolis, at Khayelitsha out on False Bay beyond Mitchells Plain (for location see Figure 1.2). This was promoted as 'orderly development', and represented recognition of the permanence of large numbers of Blacks in the Western Cape (and abandonment of a long-standing 'Coloured labour preference' policy for this region), but in a peripheral location. Dissatisfaction on the part of formal township dwellers at the prospect of relocation to Khayelitsha led this element of the plan to be abandoned in 1985; Blacks illegally in Cape Town would, however, be permitted to build shacks at Khayelitsha (Cook, 1986).

Subsequent developments at Khayelitsha have involved both 'legal' and 'illegal' residents in the Western Cape, the former moving into basic 'core' dwellings which could subsequently be extended, while the latter build their own. By the end of the first phase in mid-1985 there were about 13,000 people living in 'core' houses and 30,000 squatters had moved from Crossroads. However, riots broke out

*Life in the shack cities: **Plate 27** (l) access to basic services such as water supply is limited; **Plate 28** (r) home is what you can make of it, as in this Crossroads shack.*

over forced removals from Crossroads in February 1985, leaving 18 dead. And in 1986 more serious disturbances occurred when conservative Blacks (known as 'witdoeke') clashed with radicals ('comrades'), with up to 100 people killed and thousands of shack dwellings destroyed. There were suspicions that the authorities had used conflict within Crossroads to help break up the settlement and encourage moves to Khayelitsha.

Today, Khayelitsha is a vast, sprawling congregation of shacks of varying quality and core houses in varying states of extension, along with areas of formal housing including small up-market enclaves. Its population is said to be a quarter of a million, with large areas laid out for further development. And on the shore of False Bay an elaborate camping and recreation area has recently been constructed, with a high quality of layout and design which contrasts starkly with the pervading lack of amenities in the settlement itself and an unemployment rate estimated at 60-70 per cent. Meanwhile, in Crossroads, there is little indication of upgrade in recent years, and long lines of tents still house some of those whose dwellings were destroyed in the riots.

The shock of seeing shack settlements in the Western Cape has been conveyed as follows by someone not unfamiliar with South Africa (Peter Hain, **The Guardian**, 3 Jan. 1990):

> We went to a squatter settlement called Brown's Farm, outside Cape Town, and the conditions there! There were no facilities at all; about 15,000 people just dumped on the sand dunes with the dust blowing into them the whole time, covering themselves, effectively trying to live under plastic bags. They were the dirtiest kids I have ever seen

> ... There was no water supply. Women are forced to walk half a mile, across a main road - where some of them have been injured while doing it - to carry back water on their heads. It is that contrast, between that and the decadence, the almost obscene affluence which you see whites live in, which has to be continually explained to the outside world.

The second case is taken from part of one of the Homelands - Winterveld in Bophuthatswana (for location, see Figure 5.1). This piece of 'independent republic' contains three formal townships but also a large population of Blacks who have settled spontaneously outside them. By the time Bophuthatswana was granted its 'independence' in 1977 it is estimated that there were about 350,000 squatters in the Winterveld, Klippan and Oskraal areas around the townships. Two important features distinguish this situation from that of Blacks in spontaneous settlements within 'White' South Africa. The first is that they are geographically separated from the outer edge of the city (in this case Pretoria), and displaced to just within the Homeland. The second is that these settlements are the responsibility of an 'independent' state. What could otherwise be an expensive inconvenience to 'White' South Africa or to the city of Pretoria is thus transferred to a 'foreign country'. As P. Smit remarked, 'One of the major challenges facing *the Bophuthatswana government* is effective administration of the expanding urban settlements' (Smith, 1982, p. 42; emphasis added).

As it happens, the Bophuthatswana government had a special problem to resolve. After independence they decreed that only their own citizens had rights to land and housing, and many non-Tswana who had settled in Winterveld were forced to move out, with

Upgrading informal settlements at St Wendolins outside Durban, assisted by the Urban Foundation: **Plate 29** *(l) block making facility;* **Plate 30** *(r) completed house.*

considerable force at times. The logic of the Homeland strategy was that they should resettle in Lebowa, KwaNdebele, or wherever their own tribe was supposed to be; thus did apartheid planning reinforce tribal identities harnessed to nationalism. Many of the non-Tswana were actually rehoused in Soshanguve, just inside the RSA, as the South African Department of Cooperation and Development (sic) was obliged to take on some of the responsibility for this perverse and unanticipated outcome of the Homeland policy.

Winterveld continued to grow, and one source suggests a population of one million in the early 1980s (Unterhalter, 1987, p. 90). However, today it is thought to be 300-400,000. Field inspection in 1989 indicated that densities in some parts have thinned, and that there has been substantial upgrading in places. There are rehousing projects undertaken jointly by the Bophuthatswana government and the South African Department of Foreign Affairs (sic), as well as islands of formal housing, amidst the sea of shacks and baked mud tracks. Not far away is the huge, modernistic National Stadium, and the Morula Sun resort and casino where visiting South Africans can enjoy pleasures not easily found at home.

The third case study of informal settlement involves greater Durban. That Durban is now reputed to be one of the fastest-growing cities in the world can be attributed to the spectacular expansion of shack settlements on its fringes. Current estimates put the total number of dwellings at about 200,000, housing 2 million people, compared with 1,731,000 in informal settlements in 1987 and 1,346,000 in 1983 (C. Fourie, in Van der Kooy, 1988, p. 39). This includes perhaps 100,000 people living in 25,000 backyard shacks in the formal townships. If, as is claimed by professionals in the field, four new 'housing starts' in every five in the metropolitan region irrespective of race are now shacks, this gives new meaning to 'conventional' housing which, for most people today, is of improvised construction. Two-thirds of the African population of the metropolitan region could now be living in shacks.

As with other cities, what used to be known as shanty towns have a long history in the Durban area. A survey in 1952 found 8000 shacks housing 67,500 people, most of them in the well-established Cato Manor community. The construction of townships for the African population led to the destruction of Cato Manor, and other smaller areas of its type, and in 1970 the shanty population was officially said to be nil. However, by 1979 air surveys revealed that over over 70,000 informal dwellings had appeared in the metropolitan region, with a population estimated to be about 500,000 Africans and 43,000 Indians. Cato Manor might have gone, but settlements of this kind were back, if not literally on the map.

Figure 5.2 gives some indication of the location of shack areas around Durban. There are about 35 distinct settlements, in four major concentrations: the Inanda area near the township of KwaMashu in the north (with about 660,000 people in 1987), the Pinetown area (180,000), the area adjoining Umlazi township in the south (420,000), and the Mpumalanga area to the west (480,000). The shack population on land within the jurisdiction of the City of Durban is about 500,000. Most of the shack areas are actually situated across the Homeland border, in KwaZulu, although they form virtually continuous physical extensions of the city of Durban and part of its broader labour market region (for those who can find work). Location in KwaZulu means that most of the informal settlements are on tribal land, for which a payment is made; they are not therefore illegal, as is usually the case in the city outside the Homelands. However, residents are subject to what is at times brutal control exercised by vigilantes acting for those who may take it upon themselves to allocate sites and collect money for them. Violence among competing political factions (see Chapter 6) adds to the pervading discomfort, insecurity and danger.

An indication of living conditions in the shack areas around Durban is provided by Table 5.5. Incomes are higher than in the rural areas, where there is very little work, but not as high as in the townships. Informal sector participation is higher in the shack areas; almost 40 per cent of households have at least one member involved, compared with 31 per cent in the townships and 24 per cent in rural areas. Access to amenities and services is more limited than in the townships, but better than in the rural areas in most respects. The main compensating advantage over the townships is that housing costs in the shack settlements are only about one-eighth of formal housing (May, 1989, pp. 62-3).

The growth of shack settlements has stimulated a public debate in South Africa on the role of informal activity in housing the growing urban Black population. The stance of the authorities was for some time extremely negative; many such settlements were destroyed by the bulldozer and their inhabitants shipped off to a Homeland. However, attitudes have changed in recent years. Interest has been aroused in the 'site-and-service' schemes which have been

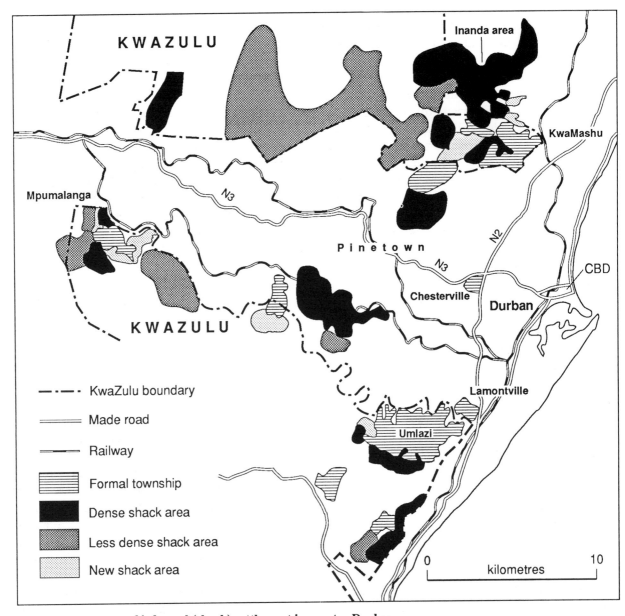

Figure 5.2   Areas of informal (shack) settlement in greater Durban
Source: The Inkatha Institute, Durban, 1986, as reproduced in Van der Kooy (1988, p. 40). Note that the areas shown are approximate and that there are differences in other sources.

adopted in some Third World countries, whereby the authorities provide land and utility lines (water and electricity) and people are permitted to construct their own dwellings, and this strategy has been applied in various places, most notably Khayelitsha. Thus spontaneous settlement is transformed from a problem to a solution to housing needs, in the hands of the people but in locations chosen and controlled by the state.

One such scheme on the fringe of Durban, which has been rehousing people from a shack area, is described as follows (May, 1989, p. 62):

There is now a fairly comprehensive infrastructure at Mfolweni, with gravel surfaced roads, stand taps which are placed every 200 metres, part prefabricated toilets

on each site and a night shift disposal system. In addition, services and amenity sites for schools, shops, churches and creches, open park spaces, reservoirs, refuse disposal and effluent disposal have been allocated. Some of these facilities have already been built, or are in the process of being built. In contrast, in Mgaga, a nearby shack settlement, the provided infrastructure consists of only eight taps ... shared by an estimated 11 000 people.

The 14,000 people of Mfolweni have clearly benefited from improved access to amenities as well as from more permanent residential rights; in fact, May describes the place as 'an enclave in which the wealthier members of the fringe population are able to enjoy a higher level of infrastructural development'.

This last point is important, for it highlights both an outcome and a constraint with respect to various kinds of shack upgrade schemes - namely that relatively few people can benefit from them. This is not merely a matter of resources, scarce as they are, but also reflects the fact that upgrading necessitates redevelopment and further population displacement. Peter Corbett, economist and member of Durban City Council, has suggested that upgrading would require up to 30 per cent of the residents of the denser areas to be relocated; thus a substantial upgrading programme around the city would involve moving up to 400,000 people. There are also organisational problems: 'The system of national, regional and local administration with respect to the shack areas is chaotic, with administrative overlapping, buck-passing, ignoring, and becoming frustrated with one another' (C. Fourie, in Van der Kooy, 1988, p. 44). To try to turn the problem of informal settlement into a solution for Black housing brings further problems, which make the solution more elusive than ever.

Changing urban and housing policy

The process of urbanisation is important in various ways, but most of all because of the involvement of a steadily increasing proportion of the Black/African population. Around half South Africa's total urban population is now Black and the Human Sciences Research Council (HSRC) has estimated that if the current rate is maintained, 75 per cent of the Black population will be urbanised by the end of the century, which means 21 million additional Blacks in urban areas by the year 2000. Not only will South Africa's

cities become steadily more Black, but their very form will increasingly be an outcome of Blacks making their own lives (shelter, work and communities) in an informal process which will become ever harder for the authorities to control unless new strategies can be devised.

Government policy with respect to Blacks in urban areas within 'White' South Africa has changed significantly in recent years. In 1977 Blacks were given some control over local affairs pertaining to their own communities, through elected councils. In 1978 a 99-year leasehold system was introduced to encourage Blacks to buy their own homes, and in 1986 this was extended to freehold. Low earnings limit demand, but prices of township houses well below market value have been used to entice Blacks of modest means into private ownership. This development was barely relevant, of course, to the mass of the Black population, who could not afford to buy, and for whom existing housing is usually overcrowded and of poor quality.

There is a sense in which Black urbanisation might be regarded not only as inevitable but also as a possible solution to other pressing problems in South Africa. Population projections by the HSRC in 1986 (and going well beyond those in Chapter 4 above) predicted a Black population of 846 million by the year 2100 if influx control constraining urbanisation continued. The Whites, along with the Indians and Coloureds, would be a miniscule minority in the total population (see Table 5.6). The abolition of influx control would reduce the figure to 132 million. But this is still much larger than the 80 million people

Table 5.5   Characteristics of Black settlements in KwaZulu/Natal

	Townships	Shacks	Rural
Average per capita income (R)	96.11	66.45	37.52
Average monthly household income (R)*	513.26	288.50	183.68
	463.63	273.56	208.40
Per cent population more than 30 minutes travel time from:			
post office	31.9	78.6	70.0
school	11.1	7.6	30.1
bus-stop	1.0	2.0	11.4
shop	3.3	3.8	23.6
water source	0.0	3.2	18.1
hospital/clinic	74.2	93.3	85.6

Source: sample surveys reported by J. May (**Indicator South Africa**, 1988, 5 (3), p. 35; 1989, 6 (1/2), p. 61); * indicates two separate surveys.

Table 5.6   **Population projections (millions) based on alternative urbanisation assumptions**

	1980	*2000*	*2050*	*2100*
Blacks, assuming that influx control:				
continues	22	37	160	846
is abolished	22	35	85	132
is abolished and Homelands industrialised	22	35	67	73
Whites	4.5	5.3	6.1	6.2
Coloureds	2.5	3.6	5.2	5.5
Indians	0.8	1.1	1.5	1.6

Source: Human Sciences Research Council, **Newsletter** 167, 1986.

which it is estimated that South Africa could actually accommodate; to restrict the population to this figure requires both the abolition of influx control and the industrialisation of the Homelands, HSRC argued.

This analysis is based on the operation of the demographic transition, whereby high birth rates and high death rates associated with low levels of economic development are replaced by continuing high birth rates but lowering death rates as 'modernisation' takes place (thus increasing natural population increase), to be followed by falling rates of birth and population increase with more advanced economic development. The key to attaining what is hoped will be a final stage of low population growth is supposed to be urban-based industrialisation, which encourages material consumption and hence population control (as took place in western Europe, for example, although evidence from the contemporary world shows that industrialisation can be accompanied by continuing high population growth). In South Africa the influx control measures

designed to prevent Blacks from swamping the cities are retarding the demographic changes on which lower rates of population growth depend. The average number of children per White woman in South Africa is approximately two, for Indians and Coloureds three, and for urban Blacks roughly four, but it is between six and seven for Black women in the Homelands. Without large-scale migration to the cities, or industrialisation in the Homelands, or both, the prospect early in the next century is for widespread poverty and famine as the Black population continues to increase ever faster.

According to the HSRC, the most effective strategy for population control thus involves industry-based metropolitan growth within or on the borders of the Homelands, as well as the continued growth of the existing metropolitan areas. The practice of industrial decentralisation is considered in the next section; attention here is confined to new developments in urbanisation policy in the heart of the Republic of South Africa.

*How some of the other one-seventh live: **Plate 31** (l) White suburb of Johannesburg, with servants' huts adjoining the houses or in the gardens; **Plate 32** (r) house in an upper-income White suburb of Cape Town, well protected from the other six-sevenths.*

*Government policy on the privatisation of Black housing, sometimes involving the clearance of shack areas, is seen as profiting developers (**Sunday Tribune**, 4 June 1989).*

It was against the background sketched out above that in 1986 a **White Paper on Urbanisation** was published, with far-reaching implications for Black settlement policy. At the same time the infamous Pass Laws responsible for influx control were repealed, a move which was widely if not universally accepted at the time as evidence of 'real reform' of a central pillar of apartheid. In their place the government proposed a policy of 'orderly urbanisation', which would supposedly apply equally to all South Africans and not only to Blacks. The state thus sought to remove the major irritant of the pass system, while still maintaining some, perhaps more selective, control of what was likely to be an accelerating process of urbanisation.

Orderly urbanisation was defined in the White Paper as, 'the freedom of movement of all citizens ... It means further that the process of urbanisation must be ordered, planned and directed by predominantly indirect forms of control, such as incentives and restrictive measures, as well as by direct measures comprising legislation and ordinances'. Direct measures included the need for Blacks to obtain 'approved accommodation', as defined by the state. Some of the controls were directed towards the containment of indiscriminate settlement with poor housing and unhealthy conditions, through the existing Slums Bill and Prevention of Illegal Squatting Act, as well as determining where housing development should take place through land use planning. The major geo-strategic significance was that the past preoccupation with keeping Blacks in the Homelands as far as possible had been replaced by attempts to channel inward migration to certain places, in particular to the metropolitan fringes.

When the euphoria surrounding the abolition of the Pass Laws had subsided, it became clear that one system of Black influx control was simply to be replaced by another. The original constraint on urbanisation was exercised in the labour market, through the need for Blacks to qualify for urban residence by employment. The new constraint was to be access to housing: new urban residents must obtain accommodation, which may be even harder to find than employment (the actual search for which may be dependent on having a place to live). Furthermore, the 7.5 million inhabitants of the 'independent' states of Transkei, Bophuthatswana, Venda and Ciskei not qualifying for South African citizenship would be treated officially as 'aliens' with respect to employment and residence in the Republic of South Africa (though this was partially relaxed under the subsequent Restoration of South African Citizens Act). Neither this citizenship criterion nor the new housing measures were explicitly racial, but they were clearly designed to control Black access to South Africa's cities.

The new significance attached to accommodation in the cities highlights the growing gap between supply and demand with respect to Black housing. Recent estimates of the shortage suggest 700,000 units outside the Homelands, including 300,000 in the PWV area alone, with the addition of almost 200,000 in the TBVC and 'self-governing territories' (SAIRR, 1989, p. 188). Table 5.7 contains estimates up to the end of the century, beginning with the 1985 housing stock for each race group and calculating the accumulating shortage arising from population growth. The magnitude of the task is indicated by the fact that the first six years of the 1980s saw only about 7700

Table 5.7   **Current and projected housing requirements 1985-2000**

Group	Housing stock		Number of housing units (1000s)			
	1985		1985	1990	1995	2000
Whites	1299	required	1262	1332	1430	1517
		shortage	*+37	33	132	218
Coloureds	394	required	446	487	538	586
		shortage	44	94	144	192
Indians	141	required	185	200	218	234
		shortage	52	60	77	93
Africans (excluding Homelands)	466	required	1004	2299	2724	3161
		shortage	538	1833	2258	2693

Source: Morkel (1987, p. 49); based on the assumption that every family and houshold has a separate home; * indicates a surplus.

housing units for Blacks built annually by the state and a little over 1000 by the private sector (figures for Whites were about 1600 and 27,500 respectively) compared with about 260,000, 85,000 and 87,000 a year required in the periods 1985-90, 1990-95 and 1995-2000 respectively, as derived from Table 5.7. It is inconceivable that increased state housing construction could bridge this gap.

The alternative to expanding state provision is more private-sector involvement. The government has been trying to encourage this, as part of its broader initiative on privatisation, deregulation and less direct controls, associated with the 'orderly urbanisation' strategy. A 'grand sale' of state-owned (ie township) housing initiated in 1983 had transferred only 58,000 units (17 per cent of the total stock) to Blacks by late 1987 (SAIRR, 1988, p. 189) but the campaign was stepped up with further inducements and by mid-1989 the figure had increased to 108,000 or 32 per cent of available stock with a further 116,000 in the non-'independent' Homelands (SAIRR, **Update**, 8, 1989, p. 18). Figures for sales of Coloured housing were 56,400 (35 per cent of state stock) and for Indians 13,200 (83 per cent).

As well as divesting itself of existing housing stock, the state has greatly reduced its role as builder. The number of units constructed fell from 7500 or so each year in the early 1980s to barely 4000 in 1987. Private-sector construction has increased, but this has been constrained by the poverty of the mass of Africans seeking a home. The Urban Foundation claims that 19 per cent cannot afford to pay anything at all towards housing and that a further 38 per cent

could afford only an 'incremental home', for example buying a serviced site and building a shack on it (**Focus on South Africa**, Nov. 1989).

Privatisation has already had a marked impact on the South African urban scene. Enclaves of expensive housing for Blacks are appearing, along with areas of more modest dwellings superior to traditional township construction. Soweto now has elite areas, such as Protea North, Pimville, Diepkloof and Dobsonville. Private purchase of state housing and its subsequent improvement adds further differentiation. In contrast are the vast swathes of shacks, themselves giving way in places to better housing as areas are cleared for private development. Private builders, anxious to acquire prime sites to serve the small but growing Black market for better housing, have been accused of corruption over land deals and of complicity in breaking up squatter communities found to be in the way. And the housing departments of the Houses of Delegates (Indians) and Representatives (Coloureds), with responsibility under the 1984 constitution for their 'own' groups, have been evicting Black squatters on land allocated for these other races. Added to all this is greater differentiation in local service provision, arising from devolution of responsibility from central authority under local government restructuring (see next section). The outcome is increasing inequality among Black (also Coloured and Indian) residential areas, within an already highly unequal society, as socio-economic status (or class) steadily augments race in determining access to a decent living environment.

Regional development planning

The new policies on urbanisation have been closely associated with regional planning, and also with the restructuring of government at local and regional scales. Together, these innovations of the 1980s are having an important bearing on emerging spatial patterns of development, which promise a geography of South Africa quite different in certain respects from the grand design of classical apartheid.

A basic feature of regional development planning in South Africa for the past three decades has been 'decentralisation'. Population migration from rural to urban areas, the disproportionately rapid growth of metropolitan regions and an increasingly polarised space economy are features of many countries, developed and underdeveloped, and state planning is usually directed towards stimulation or regeneration of the periphery and imposition of constraints on growth in the core. In South Africa the situation is given special significance by the fact that, under classical apartheid at the national scale, the core is supposed to be White and the periphery Black. The interrelated policies of influx control and decentralisation emerged in the context of the continuing contradiction between the Whites' need for cheap Black labour and the preservation of racial territorial integrity.

The use of industrial decentralisation as a strategy for keeping Blacks out of the cities was recognised as soon as the Nationalists came to power. However, government policy was initially that industrial development within the Homelands should be undertaken only with Black capital. Thus the industrial decentralisation programme established in 1960 sought to encourage development in 'border areas' or selected 'White' towns adjoining the Homelands. Black labour would be drawn from the Homelands for the most part, as an early version of the frontier commuter. Indeed, the cheap and plentiful labour provided by the Homelands, along with financial incentives (eg grants towards land, capital and housing costs and tax concessions), was the major attraction to businesses.

The limited achievements of the border-area strategy led to a change in policy, embodied in the Environmental Planning Act of 1967. This shifted the emphasis to new 'growth points' based on existing towns or cities away from the major industrial concentrations but with more growth potential than the border areas, eg Newcastle, Pietersburg and Ladysmith. The policy of disallowing White investment in the Homelands was reversed and the government launched a programme of industrial expansion within them. The perceived need for the state to exercise greater control over industrial location in certain large urban areas was expressed in measures which constrained or prevented industrial expansion involving increased employment of Blacks. In addition, the government exercised its powers over wage determination and conditions of service to sanction measures which effectively enabled employers to reduce labour costs in border areas and Homeland locations.

The two decades 1960-80 saw 113,700 new jobs for Africans created in enterprises established in the border areas and Homelands through the development corporations responsible for decentralisation. About 75,000 were in border areas, two-thirds of them in locations adjoining KwaZulu and Bophuthatswana. The balance of almost 40,000 jobs was in the Homelands. The distribution of industrial employment created through decentralisation over the period 1960-81/82 showed 38,000 within or just outside KwaZulu, and 35,000 straddled across the border of the part of Bophuthatswana north of Pretoria where Babelegi has attracted considerable investment from South African and multinational firms, and 33,000 elsewhere (RSA, 1983, p. 241; 1985, p. 246).

Against those achievements had to be set over 100,000 jobs affected by the refusal of permission for development under the Environment and Planning Act since 1968, ie potential Black jobs in the controlled (metropolitan) areas sacrificed as part of the overall decentralisation strategy. These figures suggested a geographical transfer of employment from core to periphery, rather than a net increase of jobs for Blacks in South Africa as a whole.

The failure of industrial decentralisation and economic development within the Homelands to come up to expectations brought a further reappraisal of state policy. In 1982 the government published a White Paper entitled **The Promotion of Industrial Development: An Element of a Co-ordinated Regional Development Strategy for Southern Africa**. The essence of the new policy was the identification of broad development regions covering the whole of South Africa, and the formulation of 'a coherent regional development strategy, which should be aimed at the exploitation of the full development potential of each region, including agricultural, mining, services and industrial potential' (RSA, 1983, p. 945). This was said to require 'close cooperation between the different states', ie the Homelands and residual South Africa.

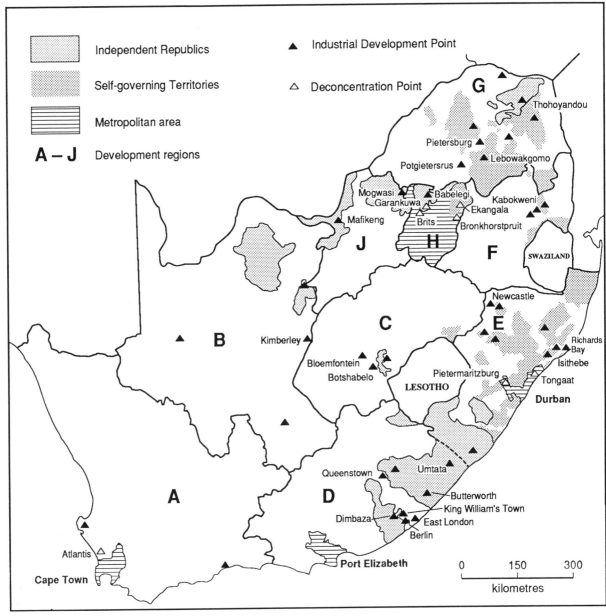

Figure 5.3   Industrial decentralisation and regional development strategy
Source: Population Census Atlas of South Africa (1986, map 8).

Figure 5.3 illustrates the main features of the new strategy. Nine (originally eight) major development regions are recognised, incorporating and in some cases splitting Homelands as well as covering the 'White' areas. The regions were classified according to relative development need, identified by the criteria of need for employment, need for higher standards of living and the potential of the region to satisfy its own employment needs. Five types of areas and/or points were distinguished: (1) metropolitan areas, with the most favourable conditions for industrial development; (2) deconcentration points, adjacent or close to the metropolitan areas, which could be used to lessen the pressure of over-concentration in the metropolitan areas; (3) industrial development points, where alternative agglomeration advantages to those in the metropolitan areas could be created so as to generate employment in the region concerned; (4) other industrial points, with less potential and/or where development needs are not as great as in other areas; (5) ad hoc cases, where decentralisation incentives may be granted if the authorities so decide.

The locations chosen for development under (2), (3) and (4) were for the most part in border areas or just inside Homelands, ie they followed a pattern similar to that of the earlier policy. Various financial incentives applied in these locations, to compensate for cost disadvantages, provide for utilities, house key personnel, and so on. Within the metropolitan areas industrial development was be controlled, but more selectively than in the past. To implement the new programmes the budget for decentralisation was doubled. Figures for 1988 show that, since the new programme was initiated in 1982, 153,000 employment opportunities had been created; jobs envisaged with respect to the 6530 projects approved amounted to 442,000, 79 per cent of them for Africans (SAIRR, 1989, pp. 343-4).

Three important features of the new strategy should be recognised. The first is that in some respects its basic intent is the same as before: to keep Blacks out of the major cities as far as possible, while at the same time facilitating their employment – hence the continuing emphasis on border-area locations and growth points just within the Homelands. The second feature is a recognition in the White Paper that the economic potential of some regions is largely of a non-industrial nature and that agriculture, mining and other forms of development would have to receive highest priority there; industrialisation is no longer a panacea for Homeland development. The third and most significant feature is that South Africa is viewed as an economically integrated territory, in which the Black so-called 'self-governing territories' and 'republics' are subsumed within the major development regions: political 'independence' clearly does not entail an independent economic identity for the Homelands.

The practice of regional development and decentralisation policy during the 1980s suggests some significant geo-strategic changes. As Rogerson (1988, pp. 235-6, 247) explains:

> while the number of growth points has been increased, the policy emphasis has moved to concentrate upon a small number of viable growth points near to the metropolitan centres or established towns. The implication of this policy shift is the concentration of resources at more economically sensible growth points which are not necessarily situated within Bantustans ... In turn, the trajectory of the programme is pointing increasingly towards short-distance deconcentration rather than the former attempt to engineer industrial growth at locations in the outermost periphery of the spatial system. ... Gone is the old-style of decentralization in support of territorial apartheid and the myth of separate Bantustan economies.

To Tomlinson (1988, pp. 495-6), the focus has changed from decentralisation to distant locations to deconcentration or 'suburbanisation' of industry,

which is intended to reinforce a deconcentrated form of urbanisation within about a 50 km radius of the cities. This interpretation has been elaborated at length in a collection of papers, in which there is reference to 'the dispersal of capital from metropolitan heartlands to metropolitan peripheries and to other regions; the enmeshing of certain bantustan labour supply areas into the process of metropolitan urbanisation': processes 'which have drained of meaning the conventional dichotomies of bantustan/ white South Africa and urban/rural' (W. Cobbett, D. Glaser, D. Hindson and M. Swilling, in Tomlinson and Addleson, 1987, p. 21).

One further ingredient has to be incorporated into the process of planned regional reformation: administrative restructuring at the sub-national scale. There are three 'tiers' of government: national, provincial and local/regional (Figure 5.4). National government has been devolving some of its responsibilities to the provinces, which in recent years have come to play an increasingly important role in the implementation of state policy on urbanisation, including Black settlement. A new system of provincial government was introduced in 1986, replacing the former White elected councils with administrators appointed by central government and executive committees, with nominated (ie not elected) multi-racial membership. This was conveyed by government as 'power-sharing', in the arena of 'general affairs' as prescribed under the 1984 constitution.

But it is in the third tier that the most significant changes have taken place, involving the establishment of Regional Service Councils (RSCs). Introduced in 1985, RSCs operate at the scale of city or metropolitan regions, to levy finance and provide such services as water, electricity, sewerage and transport, along with planning. Their official rationale is to increase efficiency, to introduce multi-racial decision-making, and to promote infrastructural development particularly in the Black, Coloured and Indian townships where the greatest need is recognised. They combine two 'reformist' strategies of depriving Whites of the monopoly on decision-making and providing for a redistribution of resources from White to black areas. Their links with other levels of government are shown in Figure 5.4.

Within the area designated as a RSC there can be up to four kinds of local government unit. These are the White local authorities, the Black local authorities established in 1982 (which are officially considered independent but attract little local support), and the

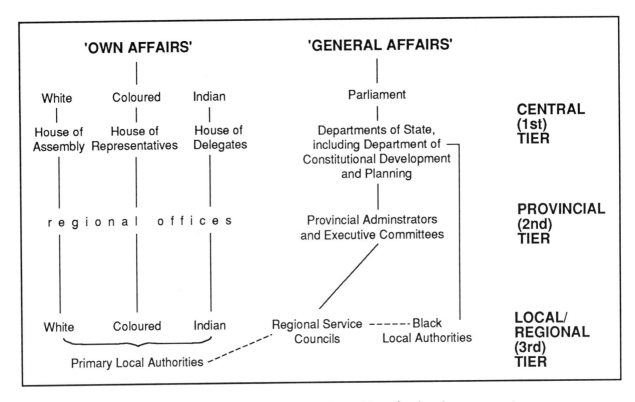

Figure 5.4   The relationship between national, provincial and local/regional government

Coloured and Indian areas where there is some local management of 'own affairs' but which are short of formal autonomy. Representation in the form of 'voting power' on the RSC is proportional to the volume of services currently purchased by a local authority, which is much larger in the White areas than the others, subject to each authority having at least one representative and none having more than half the total. A two-thirds majority is required for decisions that come to a vote.

How this local 'power-sharing' works out in one specific case is shown in Table 5.8. The Witwatersrand is covered by three RSCs, one of which is the Central Witwatersrand RSC. This has 20 members from 14 local areas which cover all four of the official race groups. Three-quarters of the total value of services is accounted for by the White local authorities and almost half by the City of Johannesburg alone. By comparison the Black areas, including Soweto, are small consumers of services, reflecting the historical neglect of township infrastructure. The table shows how this is translated into members of the RSC. The requirement that each authority is represented reduces the White members to a minority (9 of 20), but their interests are protected by the two-thirds majority criterion. As black areas are improved their voting strength will increase, but this will take time as well as redistribution of resources.

Regional Service Councils are now operating throughout South Africa, except in Natal. The legislation makes provision for incorporation of Homeland areas, as in the planning regions: a further move towards new spatial structures transcending the traditional territorial divisions of apartheid. There is obvious merit to the idea of townships across the borders being drawn into the redistributive process, but so far none has been included. The significance of the Natal case, where the extension of a Durban-based RSC into adjoining urbanised parts of KwaZulu appears so obvious, is that it has been opposed by KwaZulu; RSC boundaries excluding the Homeland have now been drawn up.

While RSCs are still in their infancy, there are reasons to doubt their efficacy as solutions to the problems of resource redistribution and multi-racial representation. Some shift of resources to black areas has taken place, but central government, the Development Bank and provincial sources provide more than ten times as much money as RSCs to the upgrading of infrastructure in black areas (1988-89 figures, from SAIRR **Update**, 8, 1989, p. 22). As political institutions they have a major problem of legitimacy, in that they incorporate the 1984 constitution's distinction between 'own' and 'general' affairs which is based on race group divisions. The role of the RSC is to make provision for certain

Table 5.8   Composition of Central Witwatersrand Regional Service Council

Area	Percentage of services bought		Members of RSC
White local authorities		74.48	9
Johannesburg	48.50		5
Roodepoort	13.04		2
Randburg	8.26		1
Sandton	4.68		1
Black local authorities		19.84	5
Soweto	12.76		2
Diepmeadow	5.34		1
Dobsonville	1.14		1
Alexandra	0.60		1
Coloured communities		2.48	3
Eldorado Park	2.18		1
Davidsonville and Fleurhof	0.12		1
Ennerdale	0.12		1
Indian communities		2.48	3
Lenesia	1.58		1
Lenesia South	0.85		1
Marlboro Gardens	0.01		1

Source: **The Regional Service Councils**, Bureau for Information, Pretoria (1988); there have been subsequent readjustments of voting power in favour of some black areas, but not enough to change the membership allocation.

'general' affairs, among racially defined local authorities which still have responsibility for their 'own' affairs. This is a long way from truly non-racial local or regional government.

In concluding the discussion of urban and regional development, it may be suggested that apartheid as a spatial planning strategy has proceeded through a number of distinct stages since the Nationalists came to power. The essential features are sketched out in Figure 5.5. Stage 1 shows the pre-apartheid pattern of ethnic diversity with some segregation in the cities, shanty towns, a large and scattered Black population in the countryside, and the reserves with their traditional subsistence economy connected to the cities by migrant labour flows. Stage 2 shows the tidying up of the social geography of the cities by the Group Areas Act and the resettlement of urban and rural Blacks into what were now deemed to be their Homelands. In stage 3 there is a distinction between two kinds of cities: those in which the Black townships may be assigned to nearby Homelands with their residents becoming frontier commuters (eg Durban) and those too far from the Homelands (eg Johannesburg) where the Black labour force must be migrants or permanent residents. In stage 3 the tidying up of the countryside continues, by eliminating 'Black spots' and furthering Homeland consolidation; informal settlements are re-emerging, with associated population removals. Stage 4 shows some borders between 'White' South Africa and the Homelands strengthened by the granting of 'independence', but this is no impediment to the continuation of established economic relations and helps to externalise some of the problems of growing informal urbanisation. Elsewhere (the city on the left in Figure 5.5), a new administrative structure is emerging, to incorporate Homeland townships and peri-urban informal settlements into the regional economy and labour market, while inforcing different levels of residential exclusion from the core city.

The interpretation of this final stage is a matter of intense debate (eg Tomlinson and Addleson, 1987; Mabin, 1989; McCarthy and Wellings, 1989). Some see it as the spatial restructuring of cheap labour

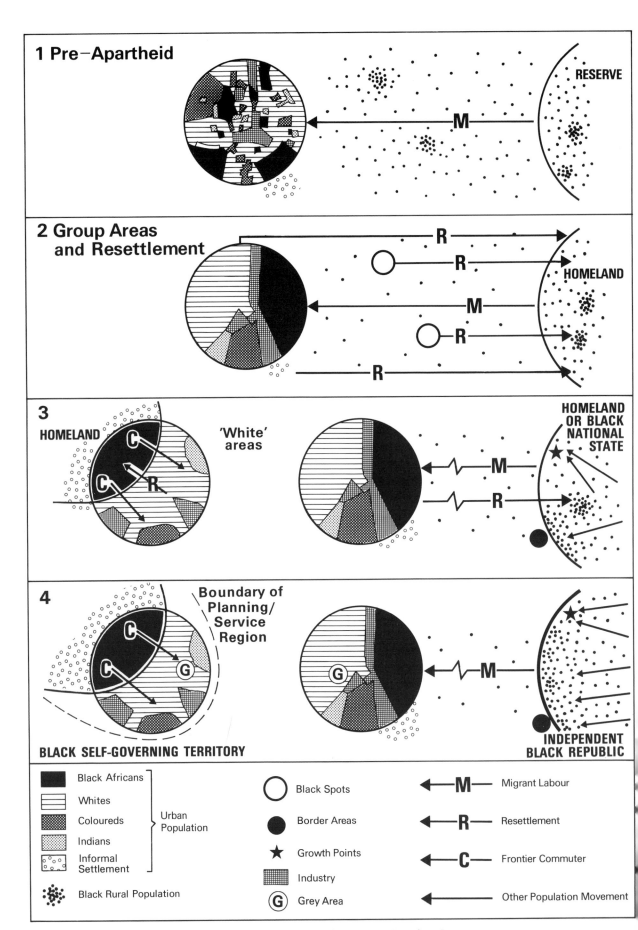

Figure 5.5 **Stages in the development and planning of urban and regional structures**
Sources: suggested in part by Western (1981, p. 65); stage 4 (right) suggested by map in **Indicator South Africa**, 3(1), 1985, p. 5.

supply, to serve the continuing interests of capital accumulation through profitable business activity. Others recognise that such things as restrictions on labour mobility and the peripheral location of much of the (black) workforce is inefficient, and thus contrary to the interests of business, and must be explained by political considerations of continued White domination. There is also some recognition that trans-racial (class) alliances may be forming at the regional level, as the well-to-do of all races find common purpose in protecting their environments and life-styles from the peripheral poor. And there is the view that planning regions and, eventually, RSCs incorporating Homelands could be a deliberately created framework for some future federal structure for a reintegrated South Africa, in which the poor/black have already been assigned a place less threatening to the (multi-racial) elite than might otherwise be the case. The spatial structure and restructuring of South Africa, like apartheid itself, does not readily yield to simple interpretations, but requires recognition of the interplay of economics and politics, race and class, in an increasingly complex society.

6 THE STRUGGLE FOR CHANGE

'Our struggle has reached a decisive moment. ...
We have waited too long for our freedom. We can
no longer wait. Now is the time to intensify the
struggle on all fronts.' (Nelson Mandela, 1990)

'For freedom dial AK-47.' (Graffiti, Lenesia, 1989)

Predicting change is risky, the more so in South
Africa where both political rhetoric and direct action
often promise more than they can deliver - and where
it is easy to exaggerate the significance of the latest
dramatic developments. Protracted if forceful
negotiation seems a more likely source of resolution
than the armed struggle symbolised by the AK-47
rifle, but no-one can be sure. Rather than trying to
foretell the future in a way that could easily be
overtaken by events, this brief final chapter looks at
two specific aspects of the struggle for change which
have attracted particular attention in recent years.
These are internal unrest or violent dissent, and
external pressure including sanctions.

Internal unrest

That apartheid should be accompanied by social
unrest is hardly surprising. However, there is more
to this than the drama of confrontations between
Blacks and the South African police or security
forces which tend to dominate media coverage. The
way in which unrest is expressed also includes less
conspicuous acts of civil disobedience or dissent
manifest both in mass boycotts of various kinds and
in individual challenges to authority or some symbol
of oppression. At the other extreme, unrest can
involve sabotage, urban 'terrorism' and the 250 or so
annual acts of insurgency reported in recent years.
The origin of unrest is also more complex than is
often supposed, with important implications for the
possible trajectory of change.

While unrest has for long been an ongoing feature of
life under apartheid, it is the major incidents that
attract most attention. The first such event was at the
township of Sharpeville on the edge of Vereeniging
in 1960 when a peaceful Black demonstration against
the Pass Laws ended in the police shooting into a
crowd, leaving 69 dead and 178 wounded. The
months that followed saw a further 83 civilians along
with 3 policemen killed, and 365 civilians and 59
police injured, in riots in various towns. A state of

emergency was declared, mass detentions were used
for the first time, and the African National Congress
was declared illegal. The 'Sharpeville massacre' has
influenced foreign attitudes to South Africa ever
since.

The second major incident, or series of incidents,
was associated with Soweto in 1976. Black discontent
over the use of Afrikaans as a compulsory medium of
instruction in schools culminated in police firing on
children, setting in motion further unrest which was
to leave about 350 dead on the Witwatersrand (Figure
6.1). Violence spread to Coloured areas of Cape
Town, where about 130 died, most of them shot by
the police. Figure 6.1 shows that the incidents of
unrest in Cape Town were spatially restricted to the
Coloured residential areas, but, unlike Soweto, they
were close enough to where Whites lived to cause
unease. There were further serious outbreaks in
1980, coinciding with the anniversary of the 1976
shootings in Soweto, but in this case events began in
the Cape and then spread to the Witwatersrand.

The latest period of heightened unrest began in
September 1984, and has continued ever since with
varying character, intensity and geographical
expression. The immediate precipitating events were
riots in Sharpeville and some Johannesburg townships
over rent increases, which resulted in about 30 deaths.
By the end of the year there were 149 deaths officially
recorded in 'political violence', in 1985 there were
879, and in 1986 a further 1300. As confrontation
between Africans and the police and security forces
escalated, accompanied by growing conflict among
blacks (including a clash between Indians and
Africans near Durban in August which left 50 dead),
a state of emergency was imposed in June 1985 in
Johannesburg and the Eastern Cape, later extended
to the Western Cape. It was lifted in March 1986, but
as violent deaths increased (to over 200 in May when
Crossroads was engulfed in conflict), a national state
of emergency was declared on 12 June along with
restrictions on the reporting of unrest. Severe press
censorship was imposed later in 1986, since when the
nature and extent of unrest has often been more a
matter of speculation than accurate reporting.

However, organisations within South Africa attempt
to monitor unrest, not least because police figures
and interpretations cannot always be relied on. The
South African Institute of Race Relations gives the
number of deaths in political conflict from September

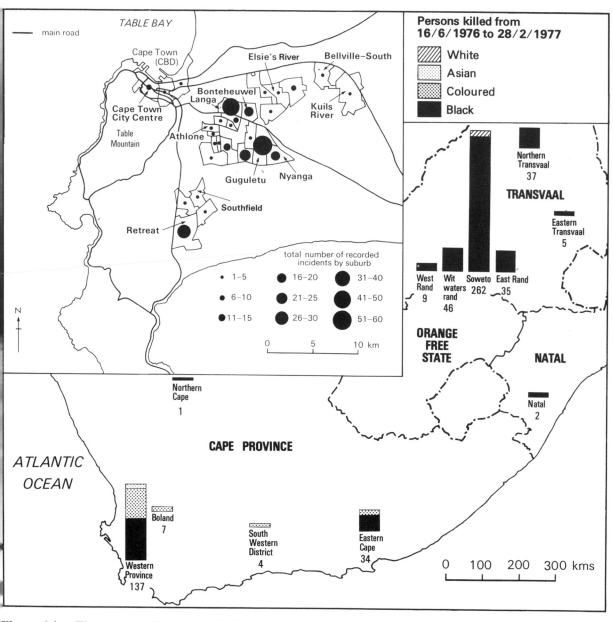

Figure 6.1   The pattern of unrest in 1976
Sources: national map from Readers' Digest **Atlas of Southern Africa** (1984, p. 34); Cape Town after J. Western (in Smith, 1982, p. 225).

1984 to the end of 1988 as 4136, very close to the 4012 provided by **Indicator South Africa.** Fluctuations over time are shown in Figure 6.2. The number of deaths went down after the national state of emergency was declared and the authorities got the situation firmly under control. However, the figure climbed again in late 1987 and deaths have subsequently remained at a level above those of the early national emergency period. This is almost entirely the result of highly localised violence, in the Pietermaritzburg area and Durban fringe, arising from conflict between radical Black political groups (the United Democratic Front, supporting the ANC) and the more conservative Zulu-based Inkatha movement (supported by the South African

government, some suspect). During almost three years up to October 1989 there were 1600 people killed in political conflict in the Natal Midlands. And the violence continues: over 50 were killed in one day in February 1990.

The fact that the trouble in Natal is not associated with an uprising against the White government emphasises the extent to which the state has regained control since 1985-86. As M. Bennett and D. Quin (Indicator Project South Africa, 1989, p. 21) explain:

after four years of intense struggle (circa 1984-88) involving a range of strategies and tactics - from violent confrontation to the

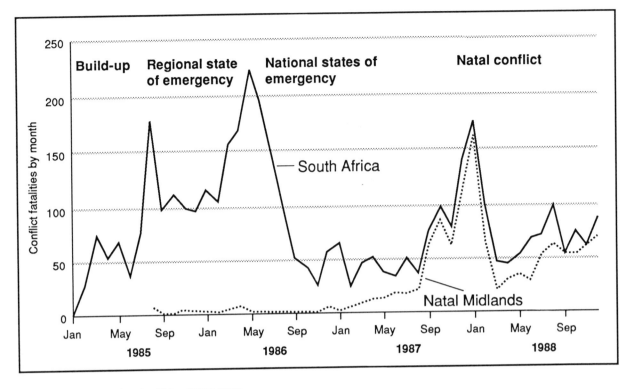

Figure 6.2   Conflict fatalities 1985-1988
Source: **Indicator South Africa**, 7 (1), 1989, p. 72.

politics of non-collaboration - the major components of the broadly defined extra-parliamentary opposition had been immobilised. Pretoria, although severely jolted by the scale and intensity of opposition, had managed to roll back the 'gains' made by various national extra-parliamentary organisations and regional civic groups, and restore the balance of power firmly in the state's favour.

It is important to recognise that, for the most part, unrest is selective with respect to both action and location. During much of 1985 and 1986 the **Cape Times** published an 'unrest map' along with the daily police reports and this provided a detailed indication of what had actually taken place. Table 6.1 lists the types of incidents and locations involved in one fairly representative month. Violent unrest usually took the form of a group of Blacks or, less often, Coloureds, throwing stones at vehicles or attacking buildings with petrol bombs. The targets were usually the South African police or defence force or institutions and individuals viewed as agents of repression. Schools were frequently attacked, sometimes by their own increasingly politicised students, as were homes and vehicles of Black policemen and local councillors and of two Coloured members of parliament. The police response was usually to move in with force, thus provoking further

violent response, and to use shotguns resulting in injuries to demonstrators. The number of Blacks killed by police action may have been larger than the 13 reported by the police themselves; there is no independent corroboration. Most of the other 19 deaths were attributed to the action of Blacks on other Blacks, including five burned to death in the 'necklace' killings involving a burning tyre which became almost a ritualised means of disposing of those considered to be informers or otherwise implicated with the forces of the state.

The types of locations involved show that the pressure points were predominantly the Black townships in 'White' South Africa. The spontaneous settlements generated only two recorded incidents of violence in this month (though they have subsequently experienced much more in the conflict in Natal). Mine compounds were the scene of four outbreaks: it is here that violence can find its most brutal expression, among men living in dormitories away from their families and with sufficient tribal loyalty for frustration to lead to vicious faction fights. The Coloured areas in the Cape erupt periodically, twice in September 1985, with a violence characteristic of that reported day to day in the Black townships. White places and people experienced very little of the violence, and the Indians, it would appear, even less (though they subsequently became targets of Black anger around Durban).

Table 6.1   Incidence of unrest in September 1985

Type of incident		Number
Attacks on vehicles:	South African police and defence force	60
	private	34
	other public and commercial	69
Attacks on buildings:	private homes	38
	schools	28
	commercial	15
	police premises	4
	other public facilities	10
Other stone throwing		28
Other violence, attacks or use of unspecified force		20
Barricades erected		10
Other arson or explosions		6
Robbery associated with unrest		5
Police use of firearms		47
Other use of firearms		5
Police use of teargas/smoke		11
Arrests made, including multiples, of:	Blacks	134
	Coloureds	45
Attacks on, injuries or woundings of:	Blacks	63
	Coloureds	8
	Whites	
	Indians	1
	Police and defence force	25
Deaths of:	Blacks killed by police action	13
	Blacks in other incidents	19
	Coloureds	2
	Police (Black)	2

Type of location	Number
Black townships in 'White' South Africa	165
Black townships in Homelands	7
Black informal settlements	2
Mines (compounds)	4
Coloured residential areas	45
White areas	12
Unidentified	6

Source: South African police daily reports, as reproduced in the **Cape Times**. Note that there is usually more than one incident reported at each location.

Violent confrontation is by no means the only strategy of opposition to White domination. There have been massive non-violent protests focused on specific issues: rent boycotts in response to the raising of rentals on overcrowded accommodation of poor quality, boycotts of buses stimulated by fare increases exacerbating the discomfort of long-distance commuting from peripheral townships, and a widespread stay-away from schools seen to provide inadequate education. There have also been highly effective boycotts of White businesses. An increase in strikes by Blacks is a further manifestation of unrest; workdays lost increased from 365,000 in 1984 to 5,714,000 in 1987 (RSA, 1989, p. 375). The

*Unrest: **Plate 33** (l) students arrested by police at a demonstration at the University of Natal in Durban, during the run-up to the 1989 general election; **Plate 34** (r) burning-tyre barricade on election day in Coloured town of Mitchells Plain,*

funerals of those killed in demonstrations have provided effective venues for mass peaceful expressions of black solidarity as well as grief.

The South African authorities attempt to portray unrest in a manner consistent with their own view of the world. State President P. W. Botha, under whose regime the uprisings of the mid-1980s took place, was quoted as saying that there is no racial strife: 'The struggle in South Africa is not a struggle between Black and White but between democratic institutions and Communist dictatorship'. Those responsible for unrest were seen as a small radical (or Marxist) minority, usually said to be affiliated with the ANC until its recent rehabilitation. Great emphasis is placed on violence by Blacks on Blacks, which government figures show to have been responsible for far more deaths than the police and defence forces.

However, there are deeper structural causes. The South African Institute of Race Relations identified the crisis in Black education (under-resourced and repressive), the economic situation (with rising unemployment) and the new constitution as underlying causes of the disturbances in 1984 which precipitated the period of heightened unrest. These specific complaints exacerbate the appalling living conditions that millions of blacks endure in townships and squatter camps. And their response is usually purposeful rather than indiscriminate, often involving the deliberate targeting of persons or property seen to be part of the system of repression.

The political scientist Lawrence Schlemmer has explained the situation as 'complex and multi-faceted', with no simple explanation: 'The events probably were shaped by an interplay of popular and spontaneous grievances, specific and systematic revolutionary influences, and a popular revolutionary

consciousness which arose as a consequence of counter-violence by the authorities' (Indicator Project South Africa, 1989, p. 36). Even in the recent Natal violence there are important causes that go beyond the ideological differences between political factions, including unemployment, and scarce resources under conditions of rapid urbanisation, setting up conflict between groups for access to the means of survival (**Indicator South Africa,** 7 (1), 1989, p. 53). It suits the government to blame radical Black politics, faction-fighting and even tribalism, for it is their policies that are at the root of unrest.

Where the South African government is right, and right to be very concerned indeed, is that the struggle is no longer exclusively racial. The antagonism between the resurgent radicalism of the ANC and more conservative elements of Black opposition reflects different views as to the heart of the problem. Blacks are increasingly seeing an exploitive capitalist economy as well as a repressive White political system as the source of their subjugation.

External pressure

External pressure for the reform or abolition of apartheid is expressed in a variety of ways. These range from exhortations and gentle encouragement to change on the part of politicians and business in some countries friendly to South Africa in certain respects (eg Britain and the United States), to assistance with the armed struggle on the part of some adjoining or nearby countries (the so-called 'front-line' states). But by far the most important, and most strenuously debated, are economic sanctions. These can take various forms, including disinvestment (ie the departure of foreign-owned firms or the transfer of their assets to others), constraints on new investment and trade embargoes.

"... a measured, step by step response ..."

*Comment on the eagerness of the British government to 'encourage' President de Klerk by relaxing sanctions against South Africa following the release of Nelson Mandela, described as a step-by-step response by Foreign Minister Douglas Hurd (**The Guardian**, 15 Feb. 1990).*

Disinvestment has increased considerably since it began in earnest towards the end of the 1970s following the Soweto uprising. During the decade up to the late 1980s, measures enacted by states, cities and other local authorities in the United States involved a total of $5 billion in disinvestment from American corporations and banks involved in South Africa. The resurgence of unrest which began in 1984 helped to precipitate the withdrawal of such well-known firms as Alfa Romeo, Coca-Cola, General Electric, General Motors, Honeywell, IBM, Kodak, Mobile, Revlon and Xerox, and the first major British departure with the sale of the South African assets of Barclays Bank in 1986.

In 1988 the United Nations identified 520 multinational companies which had sold all their equity in South Africa and/or Namibia (occupied by South Africa until recently), another 43 which had reduced their interests, and 37 in the process of disposing of equity. This compares with a reported 1267 multinationals continuing to do business in South Africa. The country of origin of the largest number of disinvesting firms was the United States with 350, followed by the UK (92), Canada (21) and

Australia with 17 (data from SAIRR, 1989, pp. 328-9). Twenty per cent of British companies operating in South Africa in 1986 left in 1987-88.

However, many of the firms which have pulled out retain non-equity ties with their former South African subsidiaries. For example, Barclays maintain strong links with the Standard Bank which took over its business. Disinvestment has therefore been to some extent cosmetic, enabling firms honestly to claim that they have no investment in South Africa while retaining some trading activity - and perhaps well placed to move back when political conditions are judged favourable.

The United States, members of the EC and other countries have imposed various other economic sanctions, including restricting trade with South Africa. Particularly significant are financial measures, which limit access to foreign capital needed for both debt repayment and investment, and force South Africa to rely more on its own resources including export earnings which can in turn be affected by trade embargoes. While the extent of compliance with sanctions on the part of individual companies and nations is variable, these measures, along with disinvestment, are thought to have exacerbated the recession in the South African economy which began in the early 1980s, resulting in slow (or no) growth, rising unemployment, and a dramatic decline in the value of the Rand.

While the South African government and its supporters sometimes dismiss the effect of sanctions, there is no doubt that they have made their mark. That this is conceded publicly as well as in private is indicated by the following extract from the 1989 budget speech of Finance Minister Barend du Plessis (quoted in **The Guardian**, 15 Feb. 1990):

> It is not unusual for a beleaguered economy to fare comparatively well to begin with. But the simple fact is that such a country's foreign exchange eventually runs out, and then - after endless damage has been done - the elementary, but remorseless truth strikes home, for both the economic and political policymakers, that no country can stand alone.

The National Party's five-year plan issued in June 1989 admitted, 'Boycotts, sanctions and disinvestment have strained the economy of the country and of every business and household'.

Sanctions have already had a detrimental impact on South Africa, substantially retarding economic growth with consequent job losses and increased poverty. Some specific predictions for the future are provided in Table 6.2. Low-intensity but escalating

sanctions would increase unemployment by 2 million by the end of the century, compared with what can be expected without sanctions. The major impact would be on unskilled jobs, in response to pressure for more capital-intensive production to increase competitiveness in exports; the numbers in skilled employment would actually be greater with sanctions than without. This suggests a particularly serious impact on Black/African employment prospects. Sanctions would reduce per capita income in all race groups, and change its distribution in favour of the Whites: the African:White ratio with sanctions is 1:3.52 compared with 1:3.04 without sanctions (calculated from Table 6.2). Savings obviously give the Whites more of a cushion against the impact of sanctions than is the case with members of other races, especially Blacks.

Of course, the South African government and businesses do what they can to minimise the negative effect. Trade sanctions have resulted in a shift in the relative importance of the country's trading partners, with London acting as a particularly important centre for the rerouteing of trade (consistent with the Thatcher government's continuing hostility to sanctions). And there have actually been positive aspects as far as South Africa is concerned: corporate disinvestment has provided opportunities for local capital to gain control of assets at less than market prices, then continue to operate the business much as before when in foreign hands (eg Barclays Bank). This has helped to consolidate the strong position of White capital, and contributes to a redistribution of wealth towards big business (Jenkins, 1989, p. 46).

Table 6.2   The possible effect of sanctions by the year 2000

Per capita income (Rand)			Employment (1000s)		
	With sanctions	*Without sanctions*		*With sanctions*	*Without sanctions*
Whites	21,688	23,358	Skilled	5,000	4,350
Indians	14,312	15,390	Unskilled	3,000	5,650
Coloureds	8,999	9,684	Unemployed	9,800	7,800
Africans	6,166	7,684			
			Total econom-		
Total	11,347	12,331	ically active	17,800	17,800

Source: R. W. Bethlehem, in **Indicator South Africa**, 1989, 6 (1/2), p. 44. The income figures exclude agriculture and domestic service, for which reliable data are not available; the employment figures include subsistence agriculture and the informal sector, and cover the RSA and TBVC area.

Not surprisingly, attitudes to sanctions vary widely. Such measures have evidently not (yet) achieved their usually stated goal of the elimination of apartheid, and this, together with their negative impact (especially on Blacks), has generated opposition in some liberal circles as well as among Blacks themselves. For example, John Kane-Berman, Director of the South African Institute for Race Relations, claims that sanctions involve great risks and very uncertain gains, and that they would slow down the pace at which the balance of economic power would shift to black people; furthermore, 'There is no doubt that sanctions, if effectively imposed, would mean more black people out of work and an increase in the incidence of malnutrition and infant mortality' (SAIRR **News**, April 1988).

However, more radical groups and much Black opinion continues to support sanctions. For example, Oliver Tambo, President of the ANC, has called again for comprehensive, mandatory sanctions (ANC leaflet, 1989):

> Sanctions are not to be seen merely as a way of reforming apartheid, nor merely as a gesture of disapproval. Sanctions are a weapon that the international community can and must use against the racist regime - a weapon that can weaken Pretoria's capacity to maintain its aggressive posture. Sanctions are a way of cutting off supply for racist South Africa and denying the regime the means through which it can sustain and perpetuate itself. ... the opposition to sanctions is based upon a determination to preserve the apartheid system.

Faced with the British government's relaxation of sanctions on investment, tourism and cultural ties so as to 'encourage' President F. W. de Klerk, Nelson Mandela had no doubt: 'We don't see any reason for a review of sanctions until a settlement is reached between the oppressed people of the country and the government' (quoted in **The Guardian**, 24 Feb. 1990). However, the ANC recognises that sanctions cannot be expected to bring down apartheid on their own; they are a complement to the wider struggle.

Given the harm that economic sanctions undoubtedly inflict on Black people, the case in favour of them is by no means straightforward, however. It could be said to rest on moral calculations as to whether short-term suffering is justified by the prospect of longer-term gains. But sanctions also act as an important symbol of support for the liberation struggle, and it is hard for opponents to show that they know better than the ANC.

Sanctions need not be confined to the economic sphere, of course, and there may be even more merit to action in other fields, For example, sports boycotts are easy to defend, on the grounds that they hurt the Whites far more than the blacks. White South African males can be fanatical about rugby football, somewhat less so but still enthusiastic about cricket, and to deprive them of access to international competition provides a potent taste of what blacks may feel when excluded from certain arenas of life including sport. 'Rebel' sports tours, heavily financed by South African business, serve as important boosters to White morale. They also reveal quite clearly that sport cannot be divorced from its social context: the English cricketers led by Mike Gatting early in 1990, for example, became pathetic pawns in the political struggle and provoked violent confrontations. There can be no 'normal' sport in an abnormal society.

Jenkins (1989, p. 46) provides a pragmatic conclusion:

> Targeted sanctions, such as the sports and entertainment boycotts have had success in peeling away some of the aspects of petty apartheid. However, sanctions targeted at the government or broad measures aimed at South Africa generally have not encouraged significant change, nor have they made more possible the toppling of the system. They appear, if anything, to have hardened conservative white attitudes, engendering a siege psychosis and prompting expressions of a fundamental unwillingness to relinquish privilege or priority.

While there is something in the argument that broad measures, including economic sanctions, may be counterproductive, it is easy to exaggerate the extent to which they encourage a defensive 'laager mentality' or even a 'backlash' among more conservative Whites. At the very least, they have required such people to recognise the revulsion towards apartheid felt in the outside world, and to understand that this has implications for their own levels of living. However, it is important to try to distinguish between action that really does have a bearing on the future of apartheid, and gestures with little practical consequence. The responsibility of those advocating or considering such measures, and those opposing them, is to consider carefully their own motivation as well as the likely outcomes.

Table 6.3   **Impact of South African destabilisation on nearby countries 1980-1988**

Country	Loss of Gross Domestic Product		War-related loss of life	
	$ million	Per cent of GDP 1988	All deaths	Infants/ young children
Angola	30,000	600	500,000	331,000
Botswana	500	40	50	-
Lesotho	300	42	500	-
Malawi	2,150	133	25,000	25,000
Mozambique	15,000	550	900,000	494,000
Swaziland	200	33	250	-
Tanzania	1,300	26	25,060	25,000
Zambia	5,000	200	50,100	50,000
Zimbabwe	8,000	145	500	-
Total	62,450	210	1,501,460	925,000

Source: United Nations (1989, p. 6).

A final aspect of external pressure is its possible impact on other parts of southern Africa. Neighbouring states carry some of the cost, as they are dependent in varying degrees on South Africa for their own prosperity, as was pointed out in Chapter 4. In particular, anything that provoked the repatriation of migrant workers, either in response to reduced economic activity in South Africa or in protection of the Republic's own citizens in times of rising unemployment, would have a dramatic effect on some of the 'front-line' states.

These states also suffer in another respect - from South African military action and deliberate 'destabilisation'. The United Nations has calculated that this cost over $60 billion and 1.5 million lives in the first nine years of the 1980s. The national distribution of these costs shows Angola and Mozambique to have suffered to the greatest extent (Table 6.3). Not included here is Namibia, which for many years was run by South Africa along apartheid lines. All these states have a strong vested interest in having a good as well as prosperous neighbour in the southern tip of the continent.

Conclusion

Internal unrest or dissent and external pressure will continue to exert an influence on the process of change in South Africa. That change is most likely to come from the people of South Africa themselves is probably right, both as a prediction and in a moral

sense. Early in 1990, a new parliament was convened (still without representatives of the Black majority of South Africa's population), with great expectations raised in some (liberal) quarters and fears in others (conservative) by President de Klerk's earlier reformist statements, the legalisation of the ANC and certain other hitherto 'banned' organisations, and the release of some political prisoners including Nelson Mandela. Meanwhile, the ANC has committed itself to continuing the armed struggle, while being drawn into negotiations over a new constitution.

In 1989, before the general election, the Nationalists had committed themselves to a five-year 'action plan for a new South Africa', with a new constitutional system in which 'no group would dominate others'. While this implies, indeed requires, Black representation, it also signals safeguards for the Whites, and for the Coloureds and Indians who might expect to fare no better under some forms of Black government than they have under the Whites. But the crucial issue is whether the Nationalists can transcend their preoccupation with 'groups', a word still virtually synonymous with race. [As long as group thinking prevails, for example in the possible addition of a fourth, explicitly Black chamber to parliament, and the preservation of the distinction between 'own' and 'general' affairs, a truly non-racial society will be impossible.]

There are signs of a rethinking of the concept of groups, to the extent of allowing for more association among those who do not want to belong to existing groups (ie a multi-racial group), and for people to move from one group to another with the consent of the recipient group. The basis of association would then become shared culture, or socio-economic status, rather than race. Such developments would recognise the fact that class affiliation is beginning to transcend race as more blacks aspire to and achieve living standards previously the privilege of the Whites.

But this kind of thinking will do no more than exasperate those (blacks and others) who see the present racial groups and cleavages as the wrong place to begin the transformation of South African society. To them, the starting point is the common humanity of all people, irrespective of race, or class, and the strong western tradition (if not necessarily practice) of equal rights under the law. This would, of course, include the right to vote, on a common electoral roll with no racial classification, and within an institutional framework where race would be irrelevant.

Black suspicions as to the sincerity of the White government, and even of its capacity to understand what is required, were voiced as follows in October 1989, at a rally to celebrate the release of some prominent political prisoners (reported in **Indicator South Africa**, 7 (1), 1989, p. 21). Walter Sisulu, former ANC secretary-general, said:

> To date, we see no clear indication that the government is serious about negotiations. All their utterances are vague. Now the government talks about ethnic elections to choose the leaders of the black people. We are looking towards the election of a Constitutional Assembly elected on the basis of universal adult franchise. This is where the true representatives of the people will discuss the future.

And Ahmed Kathrade, former member of the Transvaal Indian Congress:

> the fundamental corner-stones of apartheid still remain firmly in place. What we have seen are changes in terminology, and in this respect the Nats are past masters ... Stripped of all the nice phrases, they are simply once again changing their language and style in order to perpetuate white domination.

The truth is, of course, that there is no blank slate onto which a new non-racial society can be etched - even if its form could be agreed (capitalist or socialist, for example). History cannot be erased, and with it the way people feel and think of themselves, and of others. Nor can geography. Whatever the grand design that might emerge from a new constitutional assembly, non-racial elections, and a government in which the majority will inevitably be black, elements of the spatial structure of apartheid are bound to remain for years to come, as constraints on change. The cities will remain segregated, by occupational or political status if not by race: it will take decades to even out the quality of the inherited housing stock. The 'independent' Homelands may even survive, or some of them, if the new South Africa does not simply withdraw its financial aid. But before these and other issues can be addressed in practice, a serious process of negotiation must be engaged, with further struggle to ensure an outcome that is just.

POSTSCRIPT

Most of the revision of this publication had been completed before the un-banning of the ANC and the release of Nelson Mandela in February 1990, following President F. W. de Klerk's commitments to reform in his speech at the opening of the new session of parliament. For the first time in decades, leaders of the ANC were free to speak of their vision of a post-apartheid South Africa, and to be heard or quoted in the country itself. The months that followed have therefore clarified some of the issues which must be resolved in moving towards the abolition of the apartheid system. This Post script presents as up-to-date a view as is possible immediately before going to press in mid-1990.

The first point is that any expectation of an immediate or early end to apartheid is proving to be unfounded. The events of early 1990 were a prelude, rather than the beginning of significant change. As Mandela himself remarked at the Wembley Stadium rally to celebrate his freedom: 'The apartheid crime against humanity remains in place. It continues to kill and maim. It continues to oppress and exploit' (quoted in **The Guardian**, 17 April 1990). And he and other Blacks still have no vote in the land of their birth.

The bulk of apartheid legislation remains, and the prospect of more far-reaching change could actually constrain further reform in the short term. There is little incentive for the government to make early concessions on matters that might be the subject of future negotiations with the Blacks. De Klerk has promised to repeal the Separate Amenities Act in 1990 and said that the Group Areas Act could be amended the following year, but that the Population Registration Act used to classify South Africans by race would have to remain until a new constitution had been negotiated. He has committed himself to consult the White electorate before Blacks are given a voice in central government; the next general election is scheduled for 1994. Statements by ANC leaders, including Mandela, suggest that they also are thinking in terms of years for a new constitution to be enacted.

The preliminary talks about preconditions for constitutional negotiations began in May 1990. They had been postponed by the ANC as a protest against continuing police brutality, and the escalating violence among Black factions in Natal had provided the government with its own excuse for delay. The evident splits in Black unity, which leave the ANC (itself a non-racial organisation) by no means representative of the diversity of African opinion, are matched by the difficulty faced by the NP in conveying a White consensus in the face of right wing opposition to any significant political concessions to the Blacks. If conservative opinion can somehow be contained, it could be easier for the Whites to present a common front shared by the Nationalist and Democratic parties than to reconcile the range of Black views represented by the conservative Homeland leaders, the ANC, and the more radical Pan-Africanist Congress and Black-consciousness movements. The Whites may be able to exploit Black disunity, as well as reservations about Black/African majority rule on the part of the Coloured and Indian people - whose role in the process of change is tending to be overlooked.

The central constitutional issue is how to reconcile Black demands for one-person-one-vote, of equal value irrespective of race, with White wishes for some kind of protection from what they would regard as Black domination. De Klerk has continued to express his opposition to 'majority rule' in the generally understood sense, insisting on some special status for the White group. The Whites might be prepared to relinquish political control, while retaining the capacity to veto certain kinds of change. Thus a Black government could be acceptable if the Whites were able to block measures which seriously threatened their economic privilege and way of life. But Blacks could interpret this as the perpetuation of apartheid in the form of group advantage based on race.

Local administration, especially in the cities, could hold the key to the preservation of some degree of White privilege in a form that could be acceptable to others. Small but strong and relatively autonomous local government units controlling their own schools, police and other municipal services could serve such a purpose, while not protecting the Whites from a more redistributive form of regional and national government. Black people could move into such enclaves with the relaxation of Group Areas, if they had the money. However, anything that appears to entrench the local spatial structure of apartheid will be hard for the majority of Blacks to accept.

National reintegration involving the Homelands may be easier to achieve than the restructuring of the apartheid city. At the beginning of 1990 Transkei alone was reconsidering its 'independence', but there have subsequently been military coups in Ciskei and Venda accompanied by demands for reincorporation into the Republic of South Africa. The governments of all three of these 'republics' have now adopted a stance sympathetic to the ANC, and tensions have emerged in the hitherto conservative Bophu-thatswana. The main constitutional issue could be whether the TBVC area is to be fully merged with the RSA, swelling the number of Black voters, or whether these and the other six Homelands will be used not to exclude Blacks, as in the past, but to disperse their political power within some federal system.

That it will be impossible to disentangle political structure from economic organisation and the associated social relations is clear from preliminary verbal jousting. Mandela, Sisulu and other ANC leaders have reiterated, if at times in a muted form, their long-standing commitment to the national-isation of mines, banks and 'monopoly industry'. This they see as a necessary condition for the reorientation of the economy towards the needs of the mass of the people. The prospect of some form of socialism is as horrendous for many Whites to contemplate as Black majority rule, whereas Blacks increasingly understand that capitalist exploitation may hurt them as much as racial discrimination.

Government as well as big business and the financial institutions respond to calls for nationalisation with warnings of a threat to the economic growth on which the well-being of all South Africans depends, reinforcing their arguments with references to the demise of the planned economies of eastern Europe. Meanwhile, the state is increasing expenditure on housing and other measures to help the poor: R1000 million has been added to the R2000 million already allocated this financial year for 'the socio-economic uplift of disadvantaged South Africans irrespective of colour' (RSA Update, April 1990). The ideological commitment to free-enterprise is being tempered by pragmatism, as the impossibility of private sector solutions to the housing problem, for example, becomes increasingly obvious.

The central question linking political and economic transformation is, of course, how to tackle the extreme poverty experienced by the majority of the Black polulation. Blacks have good reason to mistrust existing economic structures as well as rejecting apartheid, and to seek more reliable redistributive mechanisms along with constitutional change. The danger in anything short of a nationwide, integrated and centrally planned strategy to combat poverty is that otherwise those Blacks who gain from political reform may be confined to the urban elite already emerging under the present process of selective incorporation. As the South African Institute for Race Relations comments (SAIRR, Update, 9, 1990, p. 4):

> The jobless, the rural poor, and the illiterate must be brought in as well. If they are not brought in from the outset we will see a new form of apartheid opening up between whites and urbanised, housed, unionised, educated blacks on the one hand, and the illiterate, malnourished, unemployed urban and rural poor on the other. Any new government in South Africa will need to be structured in such a way as to ensure that the black platteland [countryside] and the jobless all over the country are in a position to see that their needs are looked after, and not only the interests of the urban proletariat.

These sentiments are echoed and broadened by Martin Woollacott (The Guardian, 22 Feb. 1990):

> The real debate which South Africa faces is not now one about power sharing between the races, but about the delicate and dangerous balance that will have to be struck between privilege - both white privilege and class privilege generally - and the desperate and angry needs of the masses.

The abolition of apartheid, important though this is, thus constitutes only the beginning. It is the first step in a process which will require a new South Africa to confront old problems, sadly familiar to much of the rest of the world, and for which neither west nor east have yet found effective solutions.

BIBLIOGRAPHY AND SOURCES

There are numerous books and articles on South Africa, of varying quality and from different disciplinary perspectives. What follows is confined to recent geographical literature which provides an up-to-date view, sources of information used, and other material of particular relevance to recent developments discussed in this volume.

Bibliography

Beavon, K. S. O. (1982) Black townships in South Africa: terra incognita for urban geographers, **South African Geographical Journal**, 64 (1), pp. 3-20

Bernstein, A. (1989) South Africa's new city builders, **Optima**, 37 (1), pp. 18-23

Bethlehem, R. W. (1987) Time running out: structural change and policy in South Africa, **Indicator South Africa**, 4 (3), pp. 35-40

Booth, D. and Mbona, D. (1988) Leisure relations on the beach, **Indicator South Africa**, 5 (3), pp. 39-42

Cadman, V. (1986) States of independence: Sebe's Ciskei, **Indicator South Africa**, 3 (4), pp. 7-14

Centre for Policy Studies (1989) **South Africa at the End of the Eighties**, Graduate School of Business Administration, University of the Witwatersrand, Johannesburg

Christopher, A. J. (1989) Spatial variations in the application of residential segregation in South African cities, **Geoforum**, 20 (3), pp. 253-65

Cook, G. P. (1986) Khayelitsha - policy change or crisis response? **Transactions**, Institute of British Geographers, 11 (1), pp. 57-66

Davies, R. J. (1981) The spatial formation of the South African city, **GeoJournal**, supplementary issue 2, pp. 59-72

Desmond, C. (1971) **The Discarded People**, Penguin, Harmondsworth

Eberstadt, N. (1988) Poverty in South Africa, **Optima**, 36 (1), pp. 20-33

Fair, T. J. D. (1982) **South Africa: Spatial Frameworks for Development**, Juta & Co., Cape Town

Hart, D. M. (1988) Political manipulation of urban space: the razing of District Six, Cape Town, **Urban Geography**, 9 (6), pp. 603-28

Hart, D. M. and Pirie, G. H. (1984) The sight and soul of Sophiatown, **Geographical Review**, 74 (1), pp. 38-47

Indicator Project South Africa (1989) **An Overview of Political Conflict in South Africa: Data Trends 1984-1988**, University of Natal, Durban

Jenkins, C. (1989) Constructive disengagement: sanctions into the 1990s, **Indicator South Africa**, 6 (1/2), pp. 41-6

Joyce, P. (1988) **The South African Pocket Digest**, Struik, Cape Town

Lemon, A. (1987) **Apartheid in Transition**, Gower, Aldershot

Lipton, M. (1985) **Capitalism and Apartheid: South Africa 1910-84**, Gower, Aldershot

Maasdorp, G. and Pillay, N. (1977) **Urban Relocation and Racial Segregation: The Case of Indian South Africans**, Department of Economics, University of Natal, Durban

Mabin, A. (1989) Struggle for the city: urbanization and political strategies of the South African state, **Social Dynamics**, 15 (1), pp. 1-28

McCarthy, J. and Wellings, P. (1989) The regional restructuring of politics in contemporary South Africa, **Social Dynamics**, 15 (1), pp. 75-93

Mashabela, H. (1988) **Townships of the PWV**, SAIRR, Johannesburg

May, J. (1989) The push/pull dynamic: rural poverty and urban migration, **Indicator South Africa**, 6 (1/2), pp. 59-63

Moller, V. (1989) Can't get no satisfaction: quality of life in the 1980s, **Indicator South Africa**, 7 (1), pp. 43-6

Morkel, M. (1987) Black housing, **Indicator South Africa**, 4 (4), pp. 47-51

Murray, C. (1988) Displaced urbanisation, in Lonsdale, J. (ed.) **South Africa in Question**, James Currey, London, pp. 110-33

Nattrass, N. (1989) Apartheid & profit rates: challenging the radical orthodoxy, **Indicator South Africa**, 7 (1), pp. 33-7

Omond, R. (1986) **The Apartheid Handbook**, Penguin, Harmondsworth

Pickard-Cambridge, C. (1988) **The Greying of Johannesburg: Residential Desegregation in the Johannesburg Area**, SAIRR, Johannesburg

Platzky, L. and Walker, C. (1985) **The Surplus People Project: Forced Removals in South Africa**, Raven Press, Johannesburg

Rogerson, C. M. (ed.) (1986) **South Africa: Geography in State of Emergency**, special issue of **GeoJournal**, 12 (2)

Rogerson, C. M. (1988) Regional development policy in South Africa, **Development Dialogue**, 9, pp. 228-55

Rogerson, C.M. and Beavon, K.S.O. (1980) The awakening of 'Informal Sector' studies in Southern Africa, **The South African Geographical Journal,** 62 (2), pp. 175-90

RSA (annual) **South Africa,** Official Yearbook of the Republic of South Africa, Bureau for Information, Pretoria

SAIRR (annual) **Race Relations Survey,** South African Institute of Race Relations, Johannesburg

Simon, D. (1989) Crisis and change in South Africa: implications for the apartheid city, **Transactions,** Institute of Brtitish Geographers, 14 (2), pp. 189-206

Smit, P. (ed) (1985) **Black Urbanisation,** special issue of **RSA 2000,** 7 (1), Human Science Research Council, Pretoria

Smith, D.M. (1977) **Human Geography: A Welfare Approach,** Edward Arnold, London

Smith, D.M. (ed.) (1982) **Living under Apartheid: Aspects of Urbanization and Social Change in South Africa,** Allen and Unwin, London

Smith, D. M. (1987) **Geography, Inequality and Society,** Cambridge University Press, Cambridge

Stadler, A. (1987) **The Political Economy of Modern South Africa,** Croom Helm, London

Tomlinson, R. (1988) South Africa's urban policy: a new form of influx control, **Urban Affairs Quarterly,** 23 (4), pp. 487-501

Tomlinson, R. and Addleson, M. (1987) **Regional Restructuring under Apartheid: Urban and Regional Policies in Contemporary South Africa,** Raven Press, Johannesburg

United Nations (1989) **South African Destabilisation: The Economic Cost of Frontline Resistance to Apartheid,** UN Economic Commission for Africa, New York

Unterhalter, E. (1987) **Forced Removal: the Division, Segregation and Control of the People of South Africa,** International Defence and Aid Fund for Southern Africa, London

Van der Kooy, R. J. W. (1988) **Prodder's Development Annual 1988,** Programme for Development Research, Human Sciences Research Council, Pretoria

Walt, E. (1982) **South Africa - A Land Divided,** Black Sash, Johannesburg

Wellings, P. (ed.) (1986) **Southern Africa: The Development Crisis,** special issue of **Geoforum,** 17 (2)

Western, J. (1981) **Outcast Cape Town,** Allen and Unwin, London

Wolpe, H. (1988) **Race, Class and the Apartheid State,** Unesco, Paris

Zingel, J. (1985) The geopolitics of labour supply: redefining migrant boundaries in South Africa, **Indicator South Africa,** 3 (1), pp. 1-5

Sources

Most of the material presented in the Tables and Figures in this publication comes from official sources, usually those of the South African government. Much of this, along with other valuable material, is collected together in the two secondary sources, published annually, cited above as RSA and SAIRR.

The South African Institute of Race Relations (SAIRR) publishes a regular **News,** Social and Economic **Update, Quarterly Countdown** and other up-to-date reports. A subscription to the Institute (68 De Korte Street, Braamfontein, Johannesburg 2001 South Africa) is an effective means of keeping up with events.

Regular research-based articles are to be found in **Indicator South Africa,** available by subscription from the Centre for Applied Social Sciences, University of Natal, King George V Avenue, Durban, 4001 South Africa. The Centre also produces special reports on certain topics.

The International Defence and Aid Fund for Southern Africa publishes regular reports on aspects of apartheid (from Canon Collins House, 64 Essex Road, London Nl 81T).

The government of the Republic of South Africa produces a monthly **Focus** and **Update,** available from the South African Embassy (Trafalgar Square, London WC2N 5DP) free of charge.